GCSE SURVIVAL GUIDE FOR PARENTS

EMILY HUGHES

To Paul, without whom I would surely have starved to death while writing this.
Seriously, I couldn't ask for a better partner in business or in life.
Thank you for putting up with me and believing in me, all at the same time.

FOREWORD

I'm a mother of a teenager. Everyone warns you how difficult that can be, but until you're actually faced with the reality of it you can never truly understand. Every time I open my mouth I feel like I'm saying the wrong thing. My son barely speaks to me unless it's to tell me he's hungry, and not in a "Hi Mum, would you mind making me something to eat please!" kind of way.

This book is an easy read; a how-to manual to navigate the hormones and complexity of your teenager and a coping tool for the looming GCSEs. How to avoid the pitfalls and encourage your child in a supportive (and not irritating) way.

At the end of the day we all just want our children to be well adjusted human beings so they can go out into the Big Wide World and have the tools to grasp every opportunity that crosses their paths. This is a good start to that journey.

Terri Dwyer
    Producer of independent feature film Break

Acting/presenting agent
- luc@internationalartistsmanagement.co.uk

Voice agent - michele@thevoiceagency.co.uk
http://www.spotlight.com/7055-0191-4417
Www.Officialterridwyer.com
www.imdb.com/name/nm0245543/

ABOUT THE AUTHOR

5 things about Emily Hughes (in case you're interested):

1. Emily spent 15 years as a maths teacher, Head of Department and Lead Practitioner.

2. She has a degree in Mathematics with Education from Cambridge University, but she doesn't like to tell people that in case they get the mistaken impression that she's posh. She's not.

3. Emily's other jobs have included choir director, sensai, maths tutor, and shelf-stacking ninja at Our Price.

4. Emily is currently 1-2 cats away from being a crazy cat lady.

5. She is almost, but not quite, at the point where she can quote every episode of Friends verbatim.

PREFACE

After 15 (long) years of teaching maths, I'd reached the point where my own boys were doing their GCSEs, and I was surprised by how helpless I felt.

I mean, I'd been doing this forever. I was an expert in getting other people's children through their GCSEs, so why was it so different with my own?!

Turns out, it's much easier to be patient with other people's children…

I'd recently left teaching, after a few mental health wobbles caused by bureaucracy and bullies. After various not-so-awesome attempts at finding some way to replace my salary as a teacher, I'd found my choir. It was something I loved, and it paid the bills. Win!

My daughter was still in primary school. There was a Facebook group set up for the parents, and one post had really struck a chord with me.

One of the mums was pleading for help with a piece of maths homework. It was on bar modelling, which is a newish technique, so most parents hadn't even heard of it before, and she was lost.

"How do I help her with this when I don't get what they're talking about!?"

DING! Lightbulb moment.

I could combine my 15 years of teaching experience with my parenting experience, and put all the school 'stuff' into parent-friendly terms!

That's how the Parent Guide to GCSE was born.

Since then, we've helped hundreds of parents to navigate the dramas of GCSEs, and build better relationships with their children whilst doing it. ('We' now includes my husband Paul, also a teacher.)

Our membership supports parents from start to finish. We're there to hold their hands every step of the way, and we break down the information they need to know in weekly, bite-sized chunks.

It seemed like a good idea at the time to collect the basics together in a book.

I'm writing this section last, and I'd like to encourage you, should I ever suggest writing a book again, to please slap me until I see sense.

This book has been the product of a lot of late-night inspiration, enforced isolation away from distracting things like work, my children and my husband, and quite a bit of gin.

It's taken longer than I thought it would, and while I wouldn't say I'd actually *enjoyed* writing it, I haven't thrown my computer out of the window either.

I know that, despite living with two teachers, our kids still found GCSEs tough.

I've seen the effect exams have on children's mental health throughout my teaching years, and this book is my way of making your lives at least a teeny bit less stressful while *you* navigate them.

Knowledge beats nagging. Every time.

Em

INTRODUCTION

HOW TO USE THIS BOOK

I have packed this book with insights and tips gained from 15 years as a teacher and from my own experiences as a parent.

You'll probably find you get different things from it each time you read it, as things like mocks won't really feel 'real' until they get to them. That's normal.

It might even feel like a totally different book when you read it with a different child in mind. That's normal too.

In an ideal world, you'll be reading this at the start of their GCSEs.

However, if you're in a not-so-ideal world, with pandemics and school closures, a procrastinating child, or anything else that means you're starting a little later, this will still help you. And them.

Better to start late than not to start at all!

I've designed the book in stages. It will take you through from 'I don't even know where to start' to 'I know how to

help my child be ready, not just for exams, but for whatever comes next'.

You could:

- Read each stage as it becomes relevant to your child.

- Read the whole thing in one go, and then dip back in as a reference.

- Read it while you're hiding in your room with a bar of chocolate because parenting a teenager is flipping stressful.

The point is, do what works best for you.

I don't want you to feel overwhelmed by too much information in one go, because it's important to remember that all this gets spaced out over a couple of years!

At the start of each chapter, there'll be a teeny summary of what it covers, so you know where to look for things.

At the end of each chapter, there'll be a 'One Thing' to do. If you don't do anything else after reading the book except each 'One Thing', then you'll be on the right track.

Here's the basic timeline:

STAGE 1: PREPARING

This is the mental preparation bit. It talks about how your teenager's brain is developing, and why they are procrastinating.

It talks about their mindset, and finding their reason to put in the effort.

It also talks about how you can support them in developing their resilience and their independence.

(Yes, that's the 'NO MORE NAGGING' section!)

Ideally done at the very start of their GCSE journey. It can be done in advance, so the sooner you start, the better!

STAGE 2: ORGANISING

This is where you help them set up a structure for their revision, their notes, and their workspace.

This bit will probably start to happen in their first few weeks of Y10, as they start to realise what's ahead of them.

STAGE 3: STUDYING

The nuts and bolts of studying itself. Managing their time, learning how they learn best, and avoiding distractions and overwhelm.

This section is ongoing. It'll cover most of their Y10 and 11, probably up until mocks.

STAGE 4: DOING

Here's where we talk about getting them mentally ready for mocks and then for their actual exams, including tips for what to do in those stressful weeks once exams start.

This section covers mocks and final exams.

STAGE 5: WINNING

By the time you get to this stage, exams will be over.

You can all go and sun yourselves on a beach for a while, safe in the knowledge that you did everything you could.

(And then you get to do it all again for post-16…. Sorry!)

Bonus tips

We go into detail about their options not just at post-16, but also once they 'leave school', because the sooner they start thinking about what happens after school, the longer they'll have to prepare for it.

It's a great one to look at early, so if you're planning on reading through this gradually, 'What's Next?' is the only chapter you should make an exception for and read early.

We also talk about the dangers of social media!

You might find that between the support from school and this book, you're happy getting through these two years.

If however you'd like any further support, you can find us on Facebook to join our community of parents going through the same stuff as you.

You can also join our membership to access all our useful resources, and have us there to hold your hand through the whole thing. We only open a couple of times a year, and it's a good plan to sign up for the waiting list so you're first to hear when we open, since we have limited spaces!

Find out more at www.parentguidetogcse.com/membership-plans/

AND SO IT BEGINS

Have you ever stared down the barrel of a pile of ironing taller than you are, and seriously considered just throwing it away and seeing if anyone notices?

That's how your teenager feels about revision.

Ever started a diet with great intentions, only to end up a week later, sat on the sofa licking Dorito dust off your fingers so that you can prise the lid off the tub of ice cream?

I go back to the junk food because it's easier than rabbit food and sweating. I don't like to feel unfit, and I only notice I'm unfit when I try to exercise.

Your child doesn't like to feel stupid, and they only feel stupid when faced with a page of facts to learn about a concept they don't really understand. So they go back to the Xbox.

We mere humans tend to have the sticking power of a wet plaster. When the going gets tough, the tough… procrastinate. Or quit. Or eat chocolate.

. . .

"I couldn't do my homework because my pen ran out."
(Might have worked if I hadn't set it 5 days ago...)

"Sorry I'm late, I lost my shoe on the roof" (Yes, this is an actual, real-life example.)

In 15 years of teaching I've heard every excuse you can think of. They've ranged from the ridiculous to the heartbreaking, but *everyone* uses them.

If you knew that you'd only have to iron two things a day, you'd be more likely to do it.

If someone told you exactly what tasty food to eat when, and gave you an exercise you could do in 10 minutes a day, you'd be more likely to stick to it.

That's what this book will do for you and your child. It'll help you both survive the GCSE years with your sanity intact.

I'm going to take you through the bits that actually matter, one thing at a time.

If you want to read this in one go, fab.

If you want to read a section a month, also fab.

It's not a sprint, it's a marathon.

I can't run it for you, but I can hand you a cup of water to chuck over your head, and sometimes even sneak you off into a taxi for a mile or so.

· · ·

We'll go through the 5 stages of surviving GCSEs:

1. Preparing
2. Organising
3. Studying
4. Doing
5. Winning

Think of it like decorating a room.

You start by deciding on colours, clearing all the furniture out, and paying someone else to scrub the walls because it's boring.

You then faff around with masking tape to get straight edges, and set up your roller and paintbrush and stuff.

You do the actual painting bit. It's easy, *because you did all the boring prep work*.

You can stand in the middle of the room appreciating how fabulous a job you've done. Then go and pour yourself a large gin as a reward.

The stages have been refined by years of experience as a teacher, and then by the realisation that it's totally different when you're the parent instead.

We want the learning part to be simple, so that's why we go through the tedious organising-of-folders and setting-up-revision-plans bits. It's worth it.

· · ·

They're the same stages we take parents through in our online membership programme, because they *work*.

At the start of each 'stage', I'll explain where it'll take you from and to, although hopefully the titles are fairly self-explanatory!

You may notice that some stages are much longer than others, and that's because they just are.

It takes much more time to prepare your child mentally for their GCSEs than it does to prepare them practically.

The studying part takes what feels like forever, and the planning for the actual exams and what comes next will go by in a flash.

It's a bit like how being pregnant lasts roughly a million years, but then they're born, you blink, and suddenly they're a teenager... *sigh*

STAGE 1: PREPARING

THE TEENAGE BRAIN - EEEK

How their brain development impacts on their behaviour, and why that's important.

If it makes you feel better, all parents go through the phase of wondering what the heck they did wrong to create such a monster, feeling horrified at the way their teenager treats them/their siblings, and generally wanting to scream into a pillow.

Here's what you need to remember about this 'teenage' behaviour phase:

- It's (probably) normal
- They will be a fully functional human being again at the end of it
- Wine/chocolate/ice-cream helps (you, not them.)

Seriously though, it's a frustrating thing to watch as a parent. Your well-adjusted, loving child is a distant memory. You're fighting battles on a daily basis on subjects ranging from skirt length to Xbox usage to curfews.

They make decisions that we don't understand and get angry and argumentative at the drop of a hat. You don't know where this behaviour came from.

The diagnosis? You've got a case of the teenager. And there's no cure.

I could get really science-y on you here, but I'll keep it straightforward.

Your child's brain is having a massive growth spurt. It's doing all sorts of vital development that turns your child into an adult. That takes time. And patience. (Oh so much patience...)

The (slightly) science-y bit:
Meet some important bits of your brain:

The **nucleus accumbens** is all about seeking pleasure and rewards.

Think of it as your 'happy' drunk[1] friend. The one who suggests the dodgy kebab place at the end of the night (even after what happened last time...). The same one who has to be talked out of getting a tattoo/snogging someone random/drunk-texting an ex.

Basically, if left unsupervised, the nucleus accumbens will make some very questionable choices.

The **amygdala** is the place where your 'gut' reactions come from – like fear and aggression.

You know the guy who gets a bit trigger-happy when he's had a few? Who'll start a fight because someone 'looked at them funny'? That's the amygdala.

The **prefrontal cortex** handles your complex decision making.

It's the designated driver of your brain. It looks out for the drunk friends and stops them doing anything too stupid. It makes plans, controls impulses, and can actually focus on what's important in a situation.

Hang on, what's all this got to do with my teenager?

The brain goes through a big clearout when you're in your teens. It's a bit like their bedroom – it wants to get rid of anything it doesn't need any more (you know, the 'babyish' stuff), and make space for the new, grown-up stuff.

The brain does this by pruning away old connections (synapses). That lets the useful connections work better.

As the brain develops, it starts at the back, and works its way forward. It clears out the old, unused synapses, and builds up the new.

That means that the nucleus accumbens and the amygdala are being developed before the prefrontal cortex.

Yup, your drunk friends are being left unsupervised on a weekend in Vegas. Be afraid.

In a teenager, this often means putting reward over risk, or misinterpreting situations.

For example:

- Leaving your coursework until the last minute because you were out with your mates all summer

- Doing your homework on the way to school because you got distracted by a Netflix binge last night
- Not doing something your dad asked you to because your phone was more interesting.
- Having a tantrum because your mum asked you to do something 'unreasonable' – like tidy your room, brush your teeth, get off the sofa today, that kind of thing.

Anything else I should know?

We've not even mentioned the dreaded hormones yet, have we?!

As we all learned at school, you have a massive surge of hormones during puberty, and these don't just drive the physical changes. Oh no.

Ladies, I know I'm not alone in that I can be a tad bit irrational or irritable once a month.

I've had a couple of decades to get used to how this hormone imbalance affects my mood, and yet I'm still not capable of stopping it. (If you've got any secret tips, let me know!)

I know enough to warn my husband to batten down the hatches. For a teenager though, this is the first time they've dealt with this emotional rollercoaster, and theirs lasts WAY longer.

Take a second to think back to when you were a teenager. What did you argue with your parents about? Would you be on the other side of that argument now as a parent? What questionable choices did you make that you now look back on with shame….?

We've all been through it, but it's very different looking at it from the outside!

So what am I supposed to do??

Firstly, remind yourself on a daily basis not to take this personally.

It's hard to do that when doors are slamming, or your teenager hasn't actually said a word to you for days, but it really isn't about you (most of the time).

If you can, try to keep communication lines open by picking your battles carefully. You might not like the dyed-black hair that's appeared, but if you fly off the handle about *this*, then will they even *tell* you the big stuff?

A huge part of what they're doing is learning to be their own person. They're trying out different things to see who they are as an individual, and that means experimenting. They're going to want to shock you with things, and push the boundaries to learn what is ok, and what isn't.

Think about it like this – when you drag your drunk friend away from the bad choice they're about to make, they'll probably argue. BUT, when they wake up the following day (and have sobered up) they'll be pretty glad you stopped them.

It's going to take a while until the effects of 'teenager' wear off your child. Once they do, they'll be glad you were there to keep them safe and stop them doing anything too stupid.

It's worth the wait.

Why the science lesson? Well, first it's helpful to know it's not personal.

Second, it's helpful to know you've not just raised a super-irresponsible sloth-child, just a normal teenager.

THE ONE THING

Remember. This is completely normal.
You're doing an awesome job. I promise.

Choose your battles wisely, and don't take any of it personally.

---

1. The reason this relates to drunk friends is that alcohol reduces the activity in the next section of the brain. The sensible section. The one that is NOT running the show in a teenager…

WHY WON'T MY CHILD REVISE??

Hint: It's probably not laziness.
Why revision is a 'big scary thing'.

How many times have you put off something for aaaaaages, because it feels like it'll be a 'big scary thing' (hello tax return!), only to find when you actually start that it's less scary than you thought?

The short answer to why your child won't revise is that it feels like a big scary thing to them.

'Revision' sounds like a simple concept, but it's really not.

They could:

- Read their notes (boring and passive, not very effective, but the easiest choice)

- Mindmap
- Make flashcards (but then they've got to use them properly)
- Record their key notes to listen back to (but then they have to listen to the sound of their own voice, and who doesn't hate that...?!)
- Try questions (but then there's the real possibility that they'll end up feeling stupid because they don't know the answers yet).
- Do a quiz or make a quiz
- ..... the list goes on.

HOWEVER. For all those techniques, even when they find the 'right' ones for them, there's still a learning curve.

They still have to be able to decide which information is important, and should go in the notes.

They still have to decide which subject to do when, and which topic from within that subject.

They have to make actual DECISIONS. And the stakes are high.

That's why your child 'won't revise'. It's too scary.

If you're having the battle with your child about revision, do it with some empathy, however frustrated you are.

Imagine you're having your bathroom redone. The plumber turns up with his van full of tools, and all the various fittings and fixtures. He rips out the old bathroom, then he trips and falls and breaks his leg. Your only option is to finish it your-self. You have all his tools, enough spare time, and YouTube will teach you everything you need to know. Trouble is, if you mess it up, you have no bathroom, and you'll have to pay someone a fortune to fix it. And there's no-one free for at least 3 months. Where do you start? What do you research first? Does one thing depend on another?

That's the level of pressure you're talking about for revision. It's also the sheer scale and diversity of learning involved. They're not just being lazy - this is, for most of them, the biggest challenge they've ever faced.

The best way to start is to just START.

Get them to pick a topic from a subject (everyone has to do fractions in maths, for example), and collect together any notes they have already in their books. Failing that, google 'fractions GCSE tutorial' and see what comes up.

You'll find sites like BBC Bitesize will clearly lay out an overview of the topics within a subject – just check it against the specification for THEIR exam board (more on that later).

I can't overstate the importance of having a plan (more on *that* later too!).

Remind them to ignore everyone else.

It's no good comparing themselves with that person who started revising at the age of 7.

It's no good comparing themselves with their sibling who got 43 grade 9*s.

Have they done a bit of revision? Then they're doing better than they were yesterday.

Have they tried a past paper? Then they've learned a bit more about how the questions are structured, and about what they do and don't know. **They're doing better than they were yesterday.**

THE ONE THING

The anticipation is the worst bit, so starting is the key here. Even if they only do 5 minutes, **just get them to start**. That's the worst bit over with.

THE BATTLE IS WON OR LOST INSIDE THEIR HEAD

Why their mindset matters, and the impact of your words.

'Whether you think you can, or think you can't... You're right.'
Henry Ford

If your child decides they're not going to do well at GCSE, odds are they won't. It's easy (and common) for them to talk themselves out of doing well.

'I'm just not good at exams.'

'My memory is rubbish - I'll never remember it all, so why bother?'

'I want to be a hairdresser/footballer - I don't need GCSEs for that...'

I'd hear them **all the time** as a teacher.

The fact is, GCSEs are a 'big scary thing'. As humans, we tend to try to avoid big scary things. It's instinctive. But...

your ability to be resilient in the face of big scary things will have a huge impact on the rest of your life.

They may never need to solve an equation again once they've left school, but they'll need to learn how a system works and follow it. They'll need to be able to apply that system, sometimes a little bit creatively. It's the same skillset.

Algebra is fancy problem-solving.

English is communication skills.

History & Geography build critical thinking skills and a wider awareness of the world.

Science stops you accidentally blowing up your microwave, or helps you get that sofa up the corner stairs[1].

If they can see past the big scary exam part, and look at the skills they're developing and adding to their CV, then they're more likely to see the point in trying.

I hear you. "Okay Emily, I get it, but I barely know what my child is thinking any more - how am I supposed to help them to 'get' this??"

The biggest and best thing you can do is watch what you say. Whether they'll admit it or not, you are a huge influence in your child's life.

My biggest pet peeve as a teacher at parents' evening was the parents who'd sit in front of me, with their child, and announce 'Well, I was never any good at maths, so it's no wonder he's in the bottom set!'.

Would you announce to the world that you are really slow at reading, and have to sound words out? No! So then, why would you proudly tell people that you can't do basic sums without a calculator?! Grumble, grumble, rant....

The excuses we make for our shortcomings (because we all have them) become our children's excuses.

Excuse: 'I don't have time to exercise, I'm too busy'.
Reality: I use this one too often. I'm not too busy to binge-watch 'The Good Place', so I could easily make time to exercise. I choose not to.

Excuse: 'My teachers hate me, I'm always getting told off for nothing.'
Reality: Maybe your child talks while they're trying to teach, or distracts others who are trying to work, and that stops them doing their job. (They don't hate your child, they hate their behaviour. Only your child can change that.)

Or worse...
'I'm such an idiot! I forgot {insert random thing here}. What a moron.'
Wow. We all say this stuff to ourselves far too often. It's reinforcing the idea that if you make a mistake you're an idiot, or a failure. A simple 'oops' will do. You're human. Stop beating yourself up.

An important note: You can lead a horse to water, but you can't make him drink....

We have twins. They are chalk and cheese, sporty and academic, social and introverted, 'how can I help' and 'what's in it for me'.... and most noticeably, positive and negative. There's only so much you can do as a parent to change them - we've been trying for years to convert our very own Captain Negative, and it just won't take!

In this section, I'm going to talk about building the right mindset, where a challenge is a good thing, and you haven't failed unless you stop trying.

What do we mean by 'mindset'?

Carol Dweck is the Professor of Psychology at Stanford University.   She spends her time looking at why people succeed (or don't), and what we can do to tilt the odds in our favour.

She has a theory of two mindsets, and what difference they make to outcomes.

The idea is that your view of yourself can determine everything.

If you believe that intelligence is built-in, and that you can't improve it, then you have a 'fixed' mindset. You avoid failure at all costs, and jump straight into the 'blame game' when you do fail. You go for the safe option, not the challenge, because you might fail if it's too hard.

If you have a 'growth' mindset, you believe that you can learn and improve your intelligence. It's not a 'failure', it's something to learn from. Challenges are great, because they help us get better!

(If you'd like to hear her explain it all, she did a TED talk.)

· · ·

So what difference does a mindset make?

Dweck studied people's brainwaves while they answered tricky questions and got feedback. Some people (fixed mindset types) only cared about whether they were right or wrong. Feedback was tuned out, because they didn't care about improving if they were right, and had already filed it as a 'failure' if they were wrong.

Others (growth mindset types) cared much more about the feedback than about whether they were right or wrong. It was about *learning* for them.

Think about the last time you were challenged to do something slightly outside your comfort zone. How did it make you feel?

A fixed mindset would say that a challenge like that is terrifying. It's outside your comfort zone, so there's a good chance you're not smart enough to do it. Run away!

A growth mindset would say 'maybe I'm not smart enough to do it YET, but I'll never know if I don't try! Maybe I'll figure it out!'.

So which mindset does my child have now?

Which sounds more like them?

Does NOT cope well with losing.

Avoids anything that takes them out of my comfort zone.

"I can't do it."

"It's too hard."

"I'm stupid."

"I'm not _____ enough for that."

· · ·

or...

Can be proud of themselves, even if they don't come first.
    Loves a challenge.
    Doesn't give up easily.

So how do we use this to help our kids?
    Praise effort, not outcome. Don't use words like 'talented'
or 'intelligent', use words like 'hard-working' and
'dedicated'.
    Use the word '...yet' a lot. When they say 'I can't do it...',
add '...yet!'.

I think of it as having two little cartoon characters on my
shoulders, Tom & Jerry style.
    One is the little devil-creature. It's the voice that tells me
I'm not good enough / that was a pity-laugh / I look fat / I'm
doing a terrible job as a parent etc etc - you know the one.
The mean girl that lives in your head.
    The other is more like my best friend. She yells stuff like
"He didn't deserve you anyway!", and compliments my
outfit choices.

We tend to be a lot better at hearing the bad-voice, right?
    The good news is that you can retrain your brain not to
listen to it.

    You have to decide to change what you're going to pay
attention to, and then when you catch yourself hearing the

bad-voice, the one that makes you feel worthless and stupid, you (mentally) grab that little devil and SMUSH it. Go nuts. Cartoon frying-pan him right in the face, or acme kaboom him. It doesn't matter - it's telling your conscious and subconscious brain that we don't like that voice. We're not at home to Captain Negative!

It might sound stupid, but it really does work.

If you can get your child to do the same, and mentally correct the little voice that they listen to, it can make a gigantic difference to their mindset.

THE ONE THING

Listen to the words your child uses about their revision. Do they need to kick Captain Negative's ass?

Listen to the words you use too - praise effort, not outcome.

_____

1. (hint: pivot!!)

FINDING YOUR BIG FAT WHY

*The importance of them knowing what they're working for,
and how you/they can use this to help keep them motivated.*

When it comes to the future, most teenagers are best summed
up by a quote from Friends.

Monica: Phoebe, do you have a plan?
    Phoebe: (sighs) I don't even have a pl.

———

Knowing where they're headed can be the key to unlocking
their motivation to revise.

A friend of mine had decided to lose some weight. She
had a specific target to reach, which involved losing over two
stone, and a date by which to do it. Most of us would have
given up after the 17th time Slimming World told us we
couldn't eat the thing we wanted, or when we had a long day

at work and then had to drag ourselves off to yet another fitness class, but not her.

You see, she was losing weight for a *reason*. A big one. In order to be eligible for IVF, she had to hit this target. She knew what she was working for. (She made it too!)

Be honest, how often do we only *really* tidy the house properly when 'people' are coming over?

If you don't have a big fat WHY to do something, it often doesn't happen.

Questions to talk through with your child.

1. What do you LOVE doing? If you won a competition and got £10k a month for life, how would you spend your time? What activities do you get 'lost' in?

2. How could you get someone to pay you to do one of those things you love? Try googling 'jobs involving.....{your favourite activity} and see what comes up.

3. What qualifications or experience do you need to do that job?

4. What is the average salary for that job (if applicable)?

5. What skills do you have?

So many teenagers that we speak to haven't ever thought about this. Don't get me wrong, some have a really clear idea of what they want to do, but even then, they often haven't done the research about what qualifications they need to get there.

. . .

It's usually pretty tough to get them to list their skills, as they don't see themselves as clearly as you do, so you may need to help them do this.

Are they great at caring about others?

Are they the 'problem solver' of their group?

Do they always end up mediating/refereeing between their more…. um… 'hotheaded' friends?

Are they amazing at putting together outfits?

King/Queen of social media?

Master chef?

Are they quite the young entrepreneur?

All these things are skills that can be developed, and can help lead them towards the right career path.

In 10 years time, they'll be mid-twenties[1]. That's time to have finished university/apprenticeships etc, and be a few years into a job. Can they picture what they would like their life to be like?

My favourite bit of the goal-setting masterclass we built for our members is the bit where we go house shopping. We ask teenagers to head to Rightmove[2], and find 3 houses they'd like to be living in in 10 years time.

If they search for rental properties, they'll get a good idea of how much it'll cost them each month.

Rent shouldn't be more than 33% (one third) of their income, so they can multiply by 3 to find what their monthly salary needs to be to afford that, and then multiply *that* by 12 to find their annual salary.

99 times out of 100, that's like a giant bucket of ice-cold water to the face.

HOW MUCH??!?!?!?

They've not had to think about budgets before, and at this age, probably haven't ever had a job, so it's a shock.

Why do we do it to them? Well, much as you love them, you probably don't want them to still be living at home at 25, right?

Working out the route to their ideal career helps them focus on why exactly they need those grades at GCSE, and which subjects they have to take at post-16, and then which route to take after that.

THE ONE THING

Get them to spend some time thinking about their future.
Can they map out a path? Can they list 3 goals that will help them get what they want?
Maybe simply printing and sticking the picture of their dream house on the wall in front of their desk will help remind them why it's worth putting in the work now...

---

1. Aaaaargh! (Don't even think about how old *you'll* be...)
2. Other websites are available.

BEING LIKE A RUBBER BAND

Teaching your child how to bounce back, and to look for the positives.

Resilience is the ability to bounce back in the face of adversity.

It's tackling the messy kitchen even though you know it'll just be destroyed again later.

It's continuing to ask your child to tidy their room, even though they've ignored you the last 347 times.

But. It's also applying for another job, even though you didn't get the last 4 interviews.

It's continuing to submit your manuscript to publishers, even though you've been rejected by 12 already (just like JK Rowling did with Harry Potter…).

It's working every day on your small business, even though it's not paying the bills yet.

. . .

Resilience is one of the most important skills you can teach your child. And it *can* be taught.

Emotional resilience refers to your ability to adapt to stressful situations. More resilient people are able to "roll with the punches" and adapt. Less resilient people have a harder time with stress and life changes.

Some key traits of someone who is emotionally resilient:

- Emotional awareness. Understanding what they are feeling and why.
- Perseverance. They don't give up at a setback. They trust and keep on going.
- Takes control of their life. Doesn't blame outside forces or events. Knows that they can make the most of situations.
- Optimism. Looking on the bright side. Finds opportunities in every challenge.
- Support. Knows the value of a support system, and builds up a great one.

Things your child can do to develop resilience:

- Avoid thinking like a 'victim' of circumstances. Figure out how to take action to improve the situation instead.

In studying terms: Being proactive about making notes etc. as they go along during GCSEs, rather than complaining about how hard it all is and how they don't have enough time...

- **Talk to themselves positively. Stop listening to the negative voice in their head!**

See 'the battle is won or lost inside their head' in Stage 1.

- **Use strategies to avoid feeling overwhelmed by their emotions.**

Find something that works for them. That could be as simple as taking a deep breath and counting to 10, going to the 'happy place' in their head for a moment, or perhaps they could find some guided meditations aimed at helping them calm themselves.

- **Always look on the bright side of life!**

At the same time each day (we use dinner time) get everyone in the family to share their 'positive of the day'. Choosing to focus on the positives is a great habit to develop.

Gratitude is also a BIG DEAL for your mental health. Listing things you're thankful for is a great way to start the day.

Look how far you've come

When it all feels like it's never-ending, and there's still so far to go until they get to exams, it can be pretty disheartening.

When you're climbing a mountain, and you're exhausted, and you haven't reached the peak, you can look back down and see just how far you've come already.

Their revision plan is a great way to do that. They should

be able to look back over the weeks and weeks they've ticked off, to see just how much they've done. Ditto for their checklists.

It might not feel like they're improving, but they are.

In a karate class, every student does the same training. It doesn't matter if they're a white belt or a black belt, they mostly do the same punches, blocks and kicks.

When you are just starting, you make all the classic mistakes like bending your wrist when you punch. When you get a few belts in, it's not helpful to look up at the black belts, with their highly refined and rehearsed technique. It's helpful to look at the white belts, because you can see all the mistakes they're making. The fact you know they're mistakes means you've made progress from that point. You're better now than you were then.

———

The only person you should try to be better than is the person you were yesterday. *Tony Robbins*

THE ONE THING

You are your child's biggest role model.
It's really helpful to actually let them see when you're struggling with something, so they can watch you overcome it and not give up.

The phrase 'monkey see, monkey do' is probably overused, but it's scarily true for our kids. (Yes, that's the reason you're gradually turning into one of *your* parents, even though you vowed you wouldn't.)

What challenges have you overcome that you could tell them about?
What documentaries or biographies could they watch that demonstrate overcoming challenges?

When they have a setback, ask them 'ok, what can you *do* about that to improve the situation?'

INDEPENDENCE DAY

Why you need to stop being responsible for everything your child does.
(Hint: It's because THEY need to be responsible!)

As they have grown up, we've always been the ones responsible for *everything*. We feed them, we clothe them, we teach them to tie their laces and ride their bikes.

But.

They're now getting to the point where that's *not our job* any more.

My twin boys are now officially adults. Don't get me wrong - I'm pretty sure they're both still a 'work in progress', but at this point I have to trust that I've done the best job I can of preparing them for life.

Paul and I have always been very much of the mindset that our job is to make sure they are safe and happy.

That's it.

Anything else we manage is a bonus.

That doesn't mean we didn't spend years nagging them

about table manners, and how to treat other people, and why it's important to always do your best... but... that's not the most important thing we can do for them now.

The most important thing we can do for them is trust them.

Trust them to make the right choices.

Trust that we've set a good example (because 'monkey see, monkey do'.... Told you it was overused!).

Trust them to do the work set by their teachers (because they're the ones who'll face the consequences otherwise).

Trust them to not stay up until 2am on the Xbox after we've gone to bed.

Why? Because in a few months, it really CAN'T be our job. The twins will be at university. If they don't make the mistakes while they're in the safety of our home, our care, then they're going to make them miles away with no support system.

I'll certainly sleep better at that point knowing they've got most of the 'daft' out of their system.

My daughter asked me one day what there was for lunch. I replied "Whatever you can find!". She looked at me like I had two heads.

It was then that I realised that I'd become her lackey.

(To put this in context, she was 11 at the time. More than capable of making herself a sandwich.)

We think we're helping them by reminding them to do things, or by tidying up their stuff so they can find it when they need it, but we're not.

. . .

This is your official permission to stop being responsible for your child's day-to-day stuff.

WOOHOO!

Seriously.

If they put their phone down somewhere stupid, leave it. I'm sure they'll find it eventually, and the more painful the search, the less likely they are to do it again.

If you don't make them lunch, they'll get hungry enough to feed themselves.

If they don't do their homework in time, they'll be the ones to face the consequences at school.

I'm not saying don't *care*. You can nudge them in the right direction, but don't fall into the trap of nagging.

It doesn't work, and it'll just stress you both out.

When we interviewed James Shone from 'I can and I am[1]', he described it as the 3 B's. These struck me as being the perfect way to look at your role as a parent.

When they're small, you stand *between* them and the rest of the world. You're their protector.

When they're older, you walk *beside* them. It's a journey you're both on, together. As a team.

When they're 'proper' adults (in maturity, not just age) you are *behind* them. Supporting them when they need you, but they're leading the way.

The next most important thing? Remember they're not you.

One of the twins in particular is VERY different from me.

I'm glass-half-full. He's nobody-even-poured-me-a-glass.

I'm 'how can I help?'. He's 'why should I help?'.

I spend a lot of my time feeling like I've failed him as a

stepmum.

BUT. Actually, in his own individual way, he's an awesome human being. He's just VERY different from me.

Just because he doesn't see things like I do, doesn't mean his way of looking at things is wrong.

If we were all the same, life would be REALLY boring.

Think back for a minute to when you were a teenager. Are you doing now exactly what your parents *expected* you to be doing as an adult? For most of us, probably not!

You know as a parent that you'll love them. No matter what they end up doing.

Do they know that too?

I guess the point of all this is to say that it's ok to step back and let them do their own thing (most of the time).

They'll work this out. After all, we did.

THE ONE THING

Take a mental note for a day of how many questions you answer that you shouldn't.

"Where's my....?"
"What time is....?"
"How do I....?"

You're not Google.

---

1. https://icanandiam.com/

WHAT THE HECK ARE THE 9-1 GRADES?

Understanding the grading system, including what 'counts' as a pass nowadays.

So, the government decided to change the GCSE grading system in 2017-ish.

It used to go: U (ungraded), then G (low grade) up to A* (high grade).

It now goes: U (ungraded), then 1 (low grade) up to 9 (high grade).*

Why is this so confusing? Well, way back when, O-levels were also originally graded 1-9, but the *other way around*. 1 was good, 9 was bad!

There are a lot of very confused employers looking at CVs with the current mix of letters and numbers.

Unless you're in Wales, because you're sticking with the A-G system.

So what's a 'pass' now?

A grade 4 is a 'standard' pass. That's the minimum they're expected to achieve in English and Maths, otherwise they'll have to resit. It's roughly an old 'C', so it's likely to be what employers will look for (if they previously asked for a C).

A grade 5 is a 'strong' pass. That's what the government will be using as its performance measure for schools. That means that schools are likely to push hard if students are likely to achieve a 4, but *could* achieve a 5. It'll make a big difference to the school's headline figures.

It shouldn't matter any more to you than any other grade increase would though. A '4' is the key grade in terms of 'passing'.

How are they set each year?

A quick search on Google will tell you that there's no easy way to explain how grade boundaries are set each year. Given that the grade boundaries can make the difference between 'passing' and 'failing' each exam, why is that?

I'll save you some time – when you search, you'll find complicated documents from the government, which basically say: 'The folks at OfQual decide the grade boundaries based on a bunch of complicated things.'

Helpful, right?

So, here's the simplest way I can find to explain what they're doing.

1. **They mark ALL the exams**. All the marks from this year are collected in one big data set.

They won't do anything until they can see what the overall picture looks like for each separate exam.

2. **They look at the spread of marks compared to last year**.
Did everyone score a little bit higher this year? That might mean the exam was slightly easier, so in that case, they'd raise the grade boundaries (or vice versa).

3. **They look at the general ability of the current Y11 compared to last year.**
They base this judgement of 'ability' on previous testing (think Primary SATs). Then, they make little adjustments to the grade boundaries based on those. If this year's Y11's did a bit worse than last year's on their SATs, then maybe they're not quite as 'able', so they should bear that in mind when comparing their GCSE marks.

4. **They then map the new marks to the old marks**, and set the grade boundaries so that roughly the same % of students get each grade as last year. (With adjustments if this year's students are quite different in terms of their 'ability'.)

That means the grades students end up with are less related to how many marks they got on the paper than *how many marks they got compared to their peers*.

Combined Science is a special case

If they're doing Combined Science, it's slightly different.

It's 2 grades, as they'll have studied 2 GCSEs 'worth' of science, between the 3 fields (Biology, Chemistry, Physics).

The two grades will either be equal or adjacent - what this really means is that you can get (for example):

7-7 (a solid 7),

6-6 (a solid 6),

or inbetween, 7-6 (which could be thought of as a 7- or a 6+).

It's their way of making sure that you don't drop a whole grade if you're just a couple of marks away from the 7-7, so there's a little step in between that and a 6-6.

It's not really different, it's just that since it's worth 2 GCSEs, it's also 2 grades. They still add up all your marks and use grade boundaries. It just sounds more complicated!

THE ONE THING

Talk through your child's predicted grades with them (or target grades, or whatever they've been given). Make sure they understand that those are NOT a limit. There is nothing to say they can't get 4 grades higher than that! They're also based on them actually putting in the work, so if they're predicted 9's across the board, it doesn't mean they can slack off.

LESSONS I LEARNED FROM 'FROZEN'

Final thoughts on helping your child be mentally prepared for their GCSEs.
Yes, all the headings are songs from the movies Frozen or Frozen II. I'm that much of a Disney dork.

🎵 Into the unknown 🎵

We talked about finding your big fat WHY earlier. If they don't know what they want to do after school, it's tough to be able to look forwards, past the exams, to see why it's worth getting through them.

How many of us are lucky enough to be doing something we love so much that it barely even counts as 'work'? Unless you're incredibly lucky, or planned it out very carefully, most people just fall into a job because it's available, or seems like a good idea at the time, or they need the money, and then that's it.

Ask yourself/your child ('cos this works for adults too…) If you could do ANYTHING all day, every day, what would you pick?

Gaming? Why not develop or test games, or set up a YouTube channel dedicated to gaming that you can monetise? Marketing would be a good skill for that, so could be something you look at studying. Or media studies for that matter.

Shopping? You could be a personal shopper, a buyer for a store who chooses new lines (think Rachel in Friends).

Eating? Be a restaurant critic. A chef. The food taster for the Queen…!

Social butterfly? Be an event planner.

Sport? Try coaching, sports journalism, or be a sports photographer.

Reading? Be a book critic, a literary agent, a publisher, an editor.

. . .

Social Media addict? Become a social media manager for a brand. Learn the ins and outs of social media ads, and manage advertising for a company. Heck, you can build up *yourself* as a brand and become an influencer nowadays!

Once you have an idea of what life could look like, it's much easier to see past the pain of exams right now. It also helps with post-16 choices!

If that's not working, try motivation via what you don't want to happen.

You don't want to be having to resit your English or maths in Y12, trust me.

You don't want to be stuck in a job you hate because you didn't get the grades to do the one you love.

Remember that we humans can be pretty self-sabotaging, and failure is scary. If they're convinced they're going to fail, then it can seem less soul-destroying to simply not try. That way, it's not that they weren't good enough, it's just that they didn't bother trying. Boom. Ready-made excuse.

I used to have this on my classroom wall:

"It's ok not to know. It's not ok not to try."

Even if GCSE grades are totally irrelevant in their minds, they will be learning transferrable skills. Memory skills, communication skills, problem solving skills, critical thinking skills. It's all useful, forever. Even if they never use algebra again.

🎵 **Everyone's a bit of a fixer-upper.** 🎵

· · ·

We are all a work in progress.

I will never be done with learning new things. There will always be a new mistake to make.

It comes back to having a growth mindset.

Sometimes I'll send out an email, or put a post on Facebook that I think will really engage my readers, and … nothing. Doesn't mean I should quit, or beat myself up about how awful a writer I clearly am.

Sometimes I'll snap at the kids, or my husband. It doesn't mean I'm a terrible parent/wife.

Sometimes I just need to sit in bed and watch 4 episodes of something on Netflix in a row, while eating an entire bar of chocolate and drinking a large glass of wine. It doesn't mean I'm a slob.

There will always be times when your child is driving you crazy, and you lose your cool. Whether that means yelling, or whether that means grumbling about it in your head all day to yourself while no-one else has a clue why you're in such a mood, it's perfectly normal. Stop beating yourself up about it.

🎵 **Do the next right thing.** 🎵

If you know what you're working towards, every decision becomes a simple yes or no to this question:

"Will it get me closer to where I'm aiming for?"

THE ONE THING

Instead of getting stressed out about a bad test result, or the sheer volume of work to be done, or the fact that your child isn't doing as much work as you'd hoped… Remember. They are responsible for their learning, not you.
As the Frozen movies teach us:

Let it go.

STAGE 2: ORGANISING

DON'T MAKE ME THINK!

How to create a revision plan so simple and obvious that it's almost teenager-proof…

So, I'll be honest. I started writing this book *months* ago. And then I stopped.

There was no end in sight, other things were beckoning, and I figured it could wait.

(Read: I made an excuse and procrastinated.)

How did it finally get written? I made a plan.

Section by section, a bit at a time, with a deadline that I chose.

All I had to do to 'stay on track' was to complete a couple of sections a day, tick them off on the plan, and then relax, safe in the knowledge that I was 'on track'.

That's why your child NEEDS a revision plan.

Tiny chunks each day - even just 20 minutes - will add up to a huge amount of revision by the time they get to exams.

We kicked off the original Parent Guide to GCSE launch talking about how to build a great revision plan. Only it wasn't. It was 'how to try to build a great revision plan using the slightly iffy tools currently available, hopefully without it taking toooo long…'

So, we built our very own revision plan generator.

Gone are the days of drawing out grids with a ruler.

Never again should it take you three days, 4 different marker pens, and 6 highlighters just to create a decent plan.

Now, you can build a plan for the whole of the year in about 5 minutes. All you need is a list of subjects you're taking, and the school holiday dates.

You can use the free version of the plan here: https://www.parentguidetogcse.com/revision-planner/

(It's worth mentioning that there's a paid version with more bells and whistles, like the ability to prioritise subjects, or add weekend revision blocks, which is included for our members - just in case you really like bells and whistles.)

The plan will map out for them what subjects to do on what days. All they have to do is revise the subject they're told to and tick it off.

- They'll be able to see the progress they've made.

- It adds up the total blocks for each subject, so they can see how much they'll have done by the end.

- Once they've done their blocks for the day, that's it. Guilt-free time off. No need to justify whether they've 'done enough work today'.

- They'll be able to track their streak[1] of how many days they've done without missing any.

It's really important for everyone's sanity that you build some breathing space into the plan too. You know the saying... All work and no play makes your child... *a stroppy nightmare to live with.* Or something like that.

The key to making it the Ultimate Revision Plan? Add detail.

Don't make me think.

Imagine *you're* sitting down to revise for the day (yes, I know it's been a while, but work with me...).

Which of these two tasks are you more likely to crack on with?

a) Revise maths

b) Revise angles in parallel lines

Now, unless you really hate parallel lines, I'd imagine you said b. Why? Because you don't have to think about it.

'Revise maths' is so vague that your child could easily spend 10 minutes deciding which topic to do (and that's half a 20 minute block gone already), AND it gives them the freedom to just pick a nice easy topic that they already feel comfortable with.

. . .

For each subject and exam board, there's a specification. You can google them, but they all live on the exam board websites.

In these specifications, you'll find information about how the exams or NEAs (more on those later) will be set, the content to be covered, and plenty more.

Be careful to get the correct specification for the year your child is sitting their exam as they do change.

They can use these, or an exam-board-specific revision guide, or a textbook to create a checklist of the topics to be covered. (We think they are so powerful a tool that we've made a bank of checklists for our members.)

Here's why they're so amazing:

- They won't miss any topics out, as they can tick things off on the checklist as they go.

- They can use them to rate each topic.

Red = I don't get this still.

Orange = getting there.

Green = got it.

- It's a quick and easy reference to see what they should ask teachers about, or put extra blocks in on their revision plan.

The best one?

- They can use the checklist to map out the topics ON THEIR PLAN.

. . .

The plan you generate might say 'maths', but you can add topic-level detail to the plan so that they don't have to choose each day.

If your child is someone who is likely to find that detail too restrictive, they can choose instead to go to the checklist each day to cover whatever topic is next on there, which lets them have the wiggle room to pick easier topics on days when they're not really in the zone.

The details make the difference.

When should they start using a plan?

The real power of the revision plan is starting early, and doing little and often.

It all adds up, so if they can get in the habit of spending 20 minutes a day at the start of their GCSE courses, just writing up notes from whatever they've learned that day, they'll be miles ahead of their mates who wait until exams are looming.

It really does take a lot of the pressure off.

It's also a great way to show their teachers what they can do, and it'll mean mocks are much more meaningful in terms of the feedback you get from them.

(Our first tribe of Parent Guide to GCSE members joined us in September of 2019, so when the pandemic in 2020 meant exams were cancelled, those that had started early were a

LOT more confident about their centre-assessed grades! Just saying…)

What if we *didn't* start early…?

Don't worry. It's not too late.

Whether they're starting this at the start of Y11, or whether exams are in a few short weeks, a plan is still going to help.

Little and often may have become less 'little', but the plan will still take the mystery out of what to revise when. It'll still help them to try and cover some of everything by mapping it out. It'll still 'tell them what to do' each day.

THE ONE THING

Head over to https://www.parentguidetogcse.com/revision-planner/ now and sign up for your free account. You'll have a printable pdf revision plan for the whole year downloaded and ready to go in no more than 10 minutes. They can even add the plan to their phone calendar.

No more excuses!

---

1. Streaks - it's a snapchat thing

THE 'HOW'

How to help your child find the right revision methods for them.

I used to have to do long-ish journeys up and down the A14 (often more car park than road…), and so I got a subscription to Audible. I love a good business/self-help book, so I'd work my way through them on these journeys.

Trouble was, when I found a really great one, I'd have to buy the kindle version too.

Why? Because I process stuff better when I read it than when I hear it.

This doesn't apply to everything. I'm the reigning champion of any lyrics round in a quiz, and I can quote most episodes of Friends verbatim. But, there's something about audio books that just won't quite sink in.

There was a huge fad a while ago in teaching about using 'learning styles'. Kids were labelled visual, auditory or kinaesthetic[1] learners.

It's mostly been written off now, for good reason, but there's a lot to be said for figuring out how you learn best.

The way to work it out is to get them to think about lessons they really learned something from. What were they doing in that lesson that made the difference?

Someone we know swore by recording himself and his friends acting out the parts from the set texts for English literature, using silly voices and all.

He'd then listen back to the recordings, and it helped him learn the quotes as well as the meaning behind the words.

Someone else we know swears by mindmaps. She uses them for everything she has to learn.

Another student had a system using flashcards. She'd put them in boxes according to how well she knew them. She visited the red box a lot, the orange box regularly, and the green box rarely. The aim was to get them all into the green box.

I'd love to be able to give you a definitive answer. "Use this technique and you'll pass."

I can't. Your child has to find what works for them, which usually means trying each of the techniques out at least a couple of times.

Here's what you need to know:

- Active beats passive. Reading their notes is the easy route, but it's the least effective. It'll take much longer to learn things this way, and they'll be less likely to be able to apply the knowledge in other contexts.

- Most phones have a voice memo app. If they're not a fan of reading, they could record lots of their notes as audio files instead, and listen to them to revise. Make sure they have a good filing system for them though!

- Mindmaps help them link things. They start with a key concept in the middle, and then each branch is a separate aspect of it. They can use colours and pictures to make it all memorable. (They're such a great tool that I'd recommend your child reads 'Mind Map Mastery' by Tony Buzan[2] himself.)

- A great way to revise from a mindmap is to study it for a minute or two, turn it over, and try to recreate it on a blank sheet. They can 'peek' if they need to, but the aim is to get to the point where they can recreate the whole thing without needing to look again. That way they know it's fully memorised.

- Flashcards are great for testing, but you can also use them backwards - show the answer, and see if they can work out what the question would have been!

- Testing yourself is a really effective way to revise, but teenagers often avoid it as it makes them feel stupid if they don't know an answer.

Active vs Passive revision - picking the right methods!

Active revision is much more effective than passive revision.

Active revision is all about using and organising information; ideally making links between concepts and facts.

. . .

Passive revision is stuff like reading notes, and copying things from a textbook.

Most students tend to end up doing this kind of revision because they don't know a better way to do it. It's also the simplest and least scary method.

Trouble is, passive revision leads more to recognition than to recall. They will probably feel like they 'know' stuff, because their notes are getting familiar, and they recognise it, but when you ask them to cover up their notes and tell you all about a topic... Uh-oh.

I'm not saying there isn't a place for revising like this, but I am saying it SHOULD NOT be the only method they use.

Ways to be more active when revising:

1. Looking for underlying themes or principles.
2. Thinking about how things link together.
3. Relating what you are learning to 'real-life' situations.
4. Thinking how the solution to one problem may help you solve others.
5. Organising material into a hierarchical structure.
6. Creating a diagram or chart to represent a topic.
7. Looking for similarities or differences.
8. Looking for points for and against an argument.
9. Trying to really understand how formulae work.
10. Critically evaluating what you are learning.
11. Discussing topics with a friend.
12. Testing your knowledge with flashcards.

13. Creating quizzes to test yourself.
14. Answering past paper questions.
15. Making a mindmap.
16. Teaching someone, or getting them to quiz you.

As a parent, the best thing you can do is ask questions. Get your child to explain a topic to you - play dumb, so it feels like interest rather than interrogation. This isn't about right or wrong, this is about helping them to process the information.

Picking what works

Here are some good questions to ask when your child is trying to work out which revision techniques work best for them.

1. Write down three times where your learning has worked particularly well. They could be something you learned at school or when you've been studying independently at home.
2. Why did these learning methods work so well for you? What activities did you do to help you learn?
3. What kind of environment do you need to be in to make your learning effective? Do you need absolute quiet, gentle background noise, or to be with other people who are studying?

Habits are powerful things

One of my daily routines is that when I get up, I'll shower, then brush my teeth. Sounds obvious, but on the occasions where maybe I'm going to Pilates (which I really should do more often), I'll chuck on my workout clothes, brush my teeth and go. When I get home afterwards and shower, I'll often find myself brushing my teeth again without thinking about it. It's just that automatic!

Build a great habit

"When I …{insert daily action here}…, then I'll write up the notes from my lessons today."

My advice would be for them to do this **when they first get home from school**, but if you're not home to police it, you might prefer it to be straight after dinner instead.

The trick is to associate the actions. Whenever they get home from school, they'll do it. That way, getting home from school/eating dinner **triggers the habit**.

THE ONE THING

I've made a printable poster for revision method ideas - encourage your child to at least *try* everything on the list once. The more methods they use, the more likely they are to find what really works. Mixing up a few methods is always a better plan than doing the same (boring) thing every time.

https://www.parentguidetogcse.com/revision-methods/

---

1. learning by actually doing something physical
2. https://www.amazon.co.uk/dp/B075JNKRJZ/

THE 'WHERE'

Their work environment is important.
Here's how to set up a great one.

I went from working in a noisy classroom to working from home. With my two cats for company. It was weird, but oh so wonderfully quiet. Or so I thought…

We finally got to the point in the business where my husband could stop teaching too, and join me working from home full time. I thought it was going fantastically until one day, about two weeks in, he uttered those terror-inducing words…

"We need to talk."

Just in case I wasn't already panicked enough, he followed it up with….

.   .   .

"This isn't working."

OHMYGOSH I BROKE MY WHOLE MARRIAGE IN TWO WEEKS!

After what felt like 4 days, but was really about 4 seconds, he explained that he needed to set up an office for himself in another room. Once my heart rate had dropped back into double-digits, I asked him why, and then promptly dissolved into fits of giggles when he answered.

You see, I hadn't realised quite how much I talk to myself when I work.

Being the well-trained husband that he is, his instincts told him that when I'm talking, he should be listening, so every time I started thinking aloud, he was getting distracted from his own work!

(Long story short, we now work in separate rooms.)

Distractions are something we are going to talk about later, but first I'm going to share my biggest takeaways for setting up a workspace.

1. They might think that the sofa/bed/armchair/hammock will be comfy and so they'll learn better. Nope. What'll happen is they'll start to get backache. Use a desk or table, and a chair that supports your back.

.   .   .

2. Some people work best with music on, some with music off. I can't listen to music with lyrics when I'm writing, but when I'm doing something more artsy like designing a printable or a webpage, it actually helps me focus. There are lots of great lyric-free playlists on Spotify if they're adamant about needing music.

3. Cluttered desk = cluttered mind. When I'm feeling a bit overwhelmed with work, I tend to find that sorting out my workspace helps me clear my mind too. That said, sometimes I do that just to procrastinate[1]...

4. I've found that having a 'work space' that's separate from everything else is really helpful. It lets me switch off better when I stop work. I also find that sometimes I just can't focus where I am, and I need to go to my emergency backup workspace - for me it's the local coffee shop, where my phone reception is rubbish but they have wifi!

5. If I'm doing something important, I try to turn off my notifications. Airplane mode for the win!

I am more easily distracted than the dog from Up, and my personal 'squirrels' are Facebook and emails. If they ping up on my phone, I have to look. It's not good for my concentration[2].

Bonus tips:
Plants
If research by NASA scientists says that having house plants helps to clean the air and thus creates a better environment for working in, then this can't be bad advice, right? The

only issue is that a child's ability to remember to tidy their room is probably similar to their ability to remember to water plants... (but do NOT do it for them!)

Blackboard/Whiteboard paper

This paper is cheap, easy to apply and easy (ish) to remove. It can be used to note some of the key facts to learn, a tally of what has (or more importantly, hasn't) been revised, or just what needs to be achieved this week. It also requires zero drilling into walls.

In summary

1. Remove all distractions from the workspace.
2. Have quick and easy access to all materials.
3. Keep 'work' and 'play' areas separate.
4. No phones if possible - there are plenty of useful revision apps, but only have a phone nearby if it's for revision!
5. No internet - it's a rabbit hole they are unlikely to emerge from.
6. Brain food - important to every teenager, ever.
7. Keep it comfortable: a good chair & the right temperature.
8. Keep noise to a minimum - singing along to a tune does not help them focus on learning!
9. Ask them to note down any distractions and then help them figure out how to beat them.

THE ONE THING

Help them set up a revision space.
You can use the list above as a checklist, and then they'll need all the equipment too.

Top tip: They need to have their own (scientific) calculator, and they need to know how to use it. Borrowing one from school isn't going to cut it.
Get one that lets them type in fractions as fractions (they'll be able to show you which ones the school uses, and that's probably a good way to go).

―――――――――――――――――――――

1. ...but anything that gets them tidying is good, right?
2. Don't even get me started on TikTok.

SMARTER, NOT HARDER, FOR THE WIN

Some helpful little hacks!

Make the most of 'empty' time

If they have a journey to school, it's a great opportunity to 'hack' their time. They could listen to the set texts as an audiobook, or listen to a podcast on a subject while they walk.

If it's by car or bus, they could use one of the many great languages apps to learn some vocabulary, or use an app with flashcards or quizzes.

It's part of their day where their time is already taken, so why not make the most of it?

Make notes as they go

If they take their flashcards/notebook to school with them, they can make notes as they go along.

Maybe their break and lunch are important to them, and that's ok, but maybe they'd rather get everything done while at school, so that their time at home is spent relaxing.

. . .

Ask questions

That's what their teachers are there for!

A teacher's job is to explain the topic in a way that a child can understand. If your child doesn't understand, it's not that they're stupid (although that's what they tend to believe when it happens), it's that it hasn't been explained in a way that makes sense to them. They just need to keep asking. (Politely)

I think of it as a jigsaw puzzle. If I'm trying to put a missing piece into their puzzle, it doesn't matter how hard I try - if I'm trying to put it in upside-down, it isn't going to fit!

I have to keep trying different ways until I find the one that *does* fit.

That's why it's so important to ask questions. If a teacher can see that a student is genuinely trying to understand, they'll be happy to help. (They might be less patient if a student has spent the whole of their original explanation chatting to their mate instead of listening…. Just saying.)

Titles, titles, titles.

How frustrating is it when you're looking for something but you can't quite remember whereabouts in the book it was? Or you're looking for a jar of something in a cupboard, but the lids aren't labelled, so you have to lift each jar out to see what's in it?

Titles are a timesaver. They help you quickly identify what it is that should be on the page. It only takes 5 seconds to write one, so there's no excuse.

This goes for their schoolbooks AND for their revision notes.

Lessons are for learning

While it's both easy and tempting to spend lesson time catching up with their mates, every second they're not concentrating in lessons is time they'll have to make up at home. Simple.

Listen carefully to the kind of comments teachers make at parents' evening. Do you need to request that your child is moved away from their friend? Quite often, teenagers are reluctant to move away, or ask to be moved, in case it causes friendship dramas. You may need to offer to be the person they can 'blame' for having to move.

Have a system

Spending 10 minutes of their 30 minute block searching for where their notes are is NOT a good use of time.

Your child is going to need a system.

Here are some suggestions:

- Pinboard with folders attached, one for each subject

- Using a separate notebook for each subject

- Creating a folder with tabs for each big topic area in a subject

- Have a box for your flashcards (for one subject) with 3 sections - red, orange, green. Move the cards according to how well you understand & remember each one. Always start with the red section!

- Get 3 colours of sticky tabs (like post-its). Attach tabs to the revision guide as you've covered each section, using the red / orange / green system.

. . .

It's also a great idea to create a contents page or index.

Number the pages of the notebook, or exercise book, and leave the first/last few pages out for the contents. As you fill the book, add the title from each page to the contents.

You won't realise how big a help it is until you've stopped doing it and suddenly can't find anything!

How do I check up on their organisation system without looking like I'm nagging?

I'd approach it like this:

"I'm probably going to {insert stationery shop here} next week – while I'm there, I'd like to make sure that you've got everything you need ready for revision. Could you show me how you're organising all your notes and stuff so that I can keep an eye out for anything that'd help while I'm there?"

If they don't have a system, odds are you'll get a stroppy or non-answer.

You could then add:

"Ok, well someone showed me an article the other week about the best ways to organise revision notes – you want to pick one and I'll get the stuff?"

Then ask them if they'd rather have ring binders for each subject, notebooks, flashcards etc. Would post-its or high-lighters[1] help too?

Basically, they need notes separated by subject, then by overall topic. One size does not fit all, so they'll probably find one option appeals more than the others.

Even while you're not looking

Get them to collect posters or post-its of key facts, time-lines, mindmaps, whatever they need to learn?

They can stick them up around their room. Or the house.

For languages, they can put the German word for each item on a post-it, and stick them to the item. Or put the French word on one side of the post-it, and the English translation on the other side, so they have to turn over the post-it to check if they were right.

It may sound weird, but sticking up a poster of key facts on the wall opposite the toilet can be quite effective...

Use your words

A big part of smashing the exams is being able to understand *exactly* what the question wants.

The exams usually have a reading age of around 16.

If your child isn't a 'reader', then you might be worrying about their vocabulary, spelling and grammar.

The good news is that they can improve their vocabulary and grammar through listening, not just reading. Audiobooks are fab for this, and you can even go a step further and have all their set texts as audio books too.

If that's not working out for you, then encourage them to watch shows that are a bit more 'highbrow' than reality TV. There are some hilarious political satire shows who don't mince their words (so great for vocabulary), and so won't be too tough a sell. Beware the sweariness though.

We've got a free downloadable SPAG (spelling, punctuation and grammar) booklet with simple tips for common problems - you can grab it here: www.parentguidetogcse.com/spag-for-gcse/

Make a non-cheating cheat sheet

Let's face it – my children can barely remember where

they left their shoes. To expect them to remember every key piece of information for every subject is just crazy.

Here's the non-cheating secret. They only need to remember those final tricky facts for 10 minutes, tops.

As final preparation for an exam, get them to create a SIMPLE page with anything vital on it. They should stick to things they know they'll struggle to remember otherwise, and KEEP IT SIMPLE.

They should take the sheet with them, and sit and memorise it while they wait to go into the exam. When they get into the exam, the first thing they should do when the examiner says 'go' is to find a blank sheet of paper. Take a deep breath, and write it all back down.   BOOM! Instant fact sheet.

As they go through their revision, those facts that just won't stick will become more and more obvious. If your child starts collecting those on a cheatsheet that they revise each month, they'll make sure that only the trickiest of facts need to be on the final cheatsheet.

Little and Often - selling an early start...

It's all very well *you* knowing that your child should start making notes and revising as they go along, but how do you convince *them*?!

Well, let's say 30 minutes revision, every school day, from the start of Y10.

By the time they finish exams, (still at only 30 minutes a day here), they'll have done almost 100 hours of revision. Yes, really.

· · ·

That's equivalent to 4 weeks of 5 hours a day, 5 days a week, or a whole month's worth of work.

It also means they'll find mocks *much* easier, as they'll already have done lots of the revision.

THE ONE THING

Make sure they have a system set up for their notes.
It's down to them to pick one they think will work for them, but you may have to help them with some purchases - folders/notebooks/post-its/highlighters.

---

1. Beware 'unicorn-rainbow-highlighter-syndrome' – the overuse of so many colours, you need sunglasses to look at the flashcards. It's a common procrastination method to spend too much time making cards pretty, and too little making them useful.

   If you think this might apply to your child, just buy one colour highlighter!

STAGE 3: STUDYING

THE BIG BAD

So let's talk about the 'Big Bad'.

Procrastination.

A Master Procrastinator can spend 3 hours 'planning' very vaguely how to start work **instead of starting work**.

Tim Urban's[1] description is the best one I've found.

He describes the procrastinator's brain as being just like the non-procrastinators brain, with one exception.

Inside every procrastinator's brain there's an instant gratification monkey.

The monkey is running the show, not the sensible grown-up brain bit.

The monkey thinks it's an awesome plan to dive headfirst into a 4 hour YouTube marathon of completely random and unrelated videos.

The monkey REALLY wants you to refresh your feed on Facebook, just in case you missed anything.

The monkey only cares if things are fun.

Deadlines, shmedlines.

. . .

He says that the only thing that'll scare off the monkey for long enough to do anything useful is the Panic Monster.

'The Panic Monster is dormant most of the time, but he suddenly wakes up when a deadline gets too close or when there's danger of public embarrassment, a career disaster, or some other scary consequence.'

Sound familiar?

His top tips for beating procrastination are:
- Pick a TOP priority task. Just one.
- Break that task down into manageable chunks (really *specific* chunks)
- START! Just 5 minutes should be enough to have got past the initial 'ick' feeling.

THE ONE THING

If you have a procrastinator on your hands, you might want to get them to to watch Tim's TED talk[2] explaining all this.

Understanding what your brain is doing to you is the first step!

---

1. https://waitbutwhy.com/2013/10/why-procrastinators-procrastinate.html
2. https://www.ted.com/talks/tim_urban_inside_the_mind_of_a_master_procrastinator/transcript

10 THINGS I HATE ABOUT OVERWHELM

Why overwhelm leads to procrastination, and how to beat it.

There's a line that I love in '10 things I hate about you'.

Chastity: "I know you can be overwhelmed, and you can be underwhelmed, but can you ever just be whelmed?"
  Bianca: "I think you can in Europe."

When it comes to revision, we're aiming for 'whelmed'.
   We don't want them to be overwhelmed by the amount of work they're doing.
   We don't want *us* to be underwhelmed by the amount of work they're doing.
   Whelmed is good.
   The key to avoiding overwhelm is to break things down into manageable chunks.
   For example, I *could* have written a book five times this

length on how to help your child get through GCSEs and stay sane.

BUT, that much information would have overwhelmed you.

I kept this short and simple (and in bitesized chunks) so that you can get the basics sussed without it being a huge thing.

In our membership, we break everything down over two years, in one email a week. It means you only know what you need to know, when you need to know it, and it stops this from feeling 'too much'. Your child needs to do the same.

If they make the classic Y11 mistake of waiting until Easter to start revising, then they'll have ALL their revision to do. In one go. With exams starting in just a few weeks. (Usually around the second week of May each year.)

If they start doing little bits, even just 10 minutes a day of writing up notes, from the *start* of their GCSEs, they'll have done most of the legwork long before Easter.

While their friends are trapped inside revising frantically, they can be doing a couple of hours a day during Easter, and then catching some rays, safe in the knowledge that they're on top of all their revision.

That's why a plan is so important.

It takes away the 'where do I even start??'.

It takes away the 'how do I cover everything??'.

It takes away the guilt of 'have I done enough today??'.

Is it going to be easy? No.

Is it going to be manageable? Yes.

GCSEs are a LOT to deal with. So much of it is memory-based now that it can feel incredibly overwhelming to start thinking about revision.

Your teenager may really be totally laid back about the whole thing, but they also might be using that outer attitude to cover up for the fact that they're just really scared to start revising.

Some warning signs:

- Overuse of coloured highlighters to create the world's prettiest revision flashcards (because it can take aaaaaaaaages to do one, thus avoiding the rest!).
- Changing the subject when revision is brought up.
- The "stop nagging me – I'll do it when I'm ready!" door-slam.

A good way to diagnose whether you really need to have a chat about dealing with overwhelm, or whether you just have a lazy teen is to insist they do 5 minutes work. Just 5.

You'd be surprised at how much can be done in 5 minutes, and actually, once they've started, many will do more than 5. Starting was the scary part. (Full disclosure – this is how I get started on all my big scary jobs too!)

Those who won't even consider the 5 minutes are probably in need of a plan to beat the feeling of just having too much to do to even start.

I think the best way to explain the feeling is to tell you a story.

My daughter is possibly the least tidy person I know. It drives me C.R.A.Z.Y.

A few years ago, we extended the house a bit and now have a big den/playroom for the kids. She could wreck it in a single afternoon.

I'd be really really busy with work, and I'd be thinking 'she really ought to be the one to tidy it – after all, she made the mess, and she has to learn...!'.

But...

Then I'd get to that point where I couldn't even look at the room. It'd make my palms sweat just thinking about the state it was in. There was stuff everywhere. Parts of board games were strewn across the room, dressing-up outfits left where they'd been taken off, and wait... is that... a banana peel???? AAAAARGH!

I couldn't leave it any more. But the thought of starting? Ugh.

"This is going to take all morning. It's my day off, is this really how I want to spend it??" said the little voice in my head.

That was the overwhelm talking.

Once I'd clambered through and picked up the big stuff, it didn't look quite as scary. After I'd collected all the dressing-up clothes into their box, I could see the floor again!

With about 5 minutes of effort, it suddenly looked much more manageable.

See where I'm going with this?

THE ONE THING

Teach them the 5 minute approach to help them get over their overwhelm.

WORKIN' 9 TO 5

Why their schedule shouldn't be your schedule, the importance of taking breaks,
and how to make sure a couple of bad days don't create a problem.

I am not a morning person.

There are people who get up at 5am to get a head start on the day, who have posted their workout on Instagram already before I've even woken up. If *I* tried that, I think my whole family would move out.

I am not at my best in the mornings. It's probably fair to say that I'm not pleasant to be around before about 9am. Certainly not pre-coffee.

But that's ok. I know that. So I work around it.

I start a bit later, and I finish a bit later.

Everyone is different, so it's a good idea to get your child to set their own schedule.

You can obviously have an opinion on the amount of work

to be done, but it's much better all round if they decide for themselves *when* it gets done each day. (Just remind them that if they link the action to something they do each day, it's more likely to create a habit.)

For some, they would rather come home from school and get straight on so it's over and done with.

For others, they feel like they need a break after a full-on school day, so they'll start later.

For some, they might be 5am people who want to get up early to revise before school. (Yes, I know, stop laughing - the laws of probability say there's got to be at least one teenager in the world that applies to!)

Here's why it matters.

Firstly, as a teenager, you spend most of your time at the mercy of others. At school, you're controlled by the teachers, and the timetable. At home, it's your parents.

If you can give them the ability to decide their schedule for themselves, it's theirs to own.

They have to learn to manage their time at some point. Whether it's for university or a job, the time will come where the responsibility is theirs. Why not let them build up this skill sooner, in a safe environment?

Second, it's harder for them to argue with you when you're just reminding them of the schedule *they* decided on.

· · ·

Have a break[1]

Trying to work for 3 hours straight is not helpful. Their brain needs processing time, and will get less and less effective the longer they try to go without a break.

The Pomodoro technique is a popular way to do this:

- Set a timer for 25 minutes.

- Work your socks off (and concentrate!) until the timer goes off.

- Have a short break. Do something unrelated to work. Grab a cuppa.

This works beautifully with revision blocks too.

Each block should have a break at the end of it.

(A song is about 3-4 minutes, so they could have a mini dance break to get the blood flowing and stretch out their legs.)

If they're in the final weeks before exams, on study leave, and trying to work all day, then they should build in a longer break every 3 to 4 blocks. At least 20 minutes is best.

To weekend, or not to weekend?

Their schedule needs to be based on their circumstances.

Some have regular commitments that they have to work around. Some don't.

Some would rather do a small amount each day, some would rather do more on some days so they can do nothing on other days.

There's a lot to be said for having a full day off.

It gives them something to look forward to, and it gives them something to work for.

If they know that skipping blocks earlier in the week will

mean they have to catch them up on their day off, they're less likely to skip.

Work in weeks, not days

We all have bad days. Days where we just don't have the motivation. Days where our 'get up and go' has got up and gone.

If your child doesn't get their revision blocks done one day, it's not a problem, so long as they catch them up before the end of the week.

If they leave it too long, it starts to pile up and feel too difficult to deal with.

(It's like when you don't reply to an email straight away, and then the longer you leave it, the weirder it feels to email them back. You start to toy with the idea of pretending it went to junk so that you don't have to deal with it unless they chase it up. We've all done it.)

Quality beats quantity

Being holed up in their room all day 'revising' doesn't actually mean a lot.

If they're just passively reading their notes, or procrastinating, or being distracted by their phone, then it's not really worth it.

Too many students think that it's the hours that count.

It's not.

It's the quality of that revision time.

Going back to the tidying efforts of my daughter, she can spend 7 hours 'tidying' her room. Given that I could have done it in 10 minutes, that's pretty impressive. Or depressing.

. . .

Spending 3 hours on writing up some of their NEA isn't impressive if they spent 2 of those trying out different fonts to see which looked best.

Spending 40 minutes on a mindmap isn't impressive if they spent 30 of those doing the title in bubble writing and colouring it in.

THE ONE THING

Get your child to decide when they're going to get their revision blocks done, and when their catch-up slot is for anything they missed.

---

1. Anyone else unable to say this without mentally adding 'have a KitKat', or is it just me?

WRITING UP NOTES

Tips and tricks for getting on top of their notes

The sooner it's done, the easier it is.

Here's how it normally goes. Students do the work in lessons, then they promptly forget all about it until there's a test coming up. To prepare for the test, they go back through their school books, and any revision guides or textbooks they have, and they try and pick out key points and make notes.

Odds are, it's been months since they did it in class, so they've forgotten most of what they were taught (because they won't have written it down at the time…).

Here's a better way.

Get your child to take 5-10 minutes at the end of each school day to write up notes from that day's lessons, while they're still fresh.

This way, when they have a test coming up, they can spend their time actually reviewing and memorising things from their notes, rather than desperately trying to make the notes in the first place.

Top tips for your child when making notes:

- Make the notes on the day you learned the topic
- Add the title of the notes to the page itself, and to the contents page
- Write down key words and definitions, dates or formulae
- DON'T just copy things, write them in your own words
- Add the topic into your overview or mindmap so you can see where it fits into everything else
- RAG rate your understanding of the topic (that's Red, Amber or Green - RAG)
- File your notes if required. Don't leave them loose to get lost or mixed up!

The best possible notes have:

- A contents page or system that allows them to find their notes on any given topic straight away
- An overview of how things fit together (mindmaps are great for this)
- A way of picking out topics that need more attention (RAG rating is great for this)
- A summary at the end of a unit

- Diagrams where appropriate (visuals will help their memory)

It's also a great idea to note down anything they *didn't* understand in class. It'll help them work out what to ask their teacher or search for on YouTube to get more information.

THE ONE THING

Get your child to build in a daily habit where they spend 10 minutes writing up their notes from anything they've learned.

ESSAYS AND NEAS

A short but important explanation of what NEAs are, and how to approach them.

For those of us old enough to remember Walkmans, NEAs (non-examined assessments) are a fancy acronym for coursework.

They don't happen in every subject, but when they do, they involve preparation, planning, and actual get-your-head-down work.

It's a VERY good idea to check in with school and find out the due dates for NEAs. Teenagers aren't famed for their forward planning, so you can find yourself having the conversation about *why* exactly they're only just starting it when it's **due in 2 days** *far too easily.*

. . .

Exam boards will include deadlines for these in their exam timetables, but schools often ask for them to be submitted quite a bit earlier than that to allow time for marking, and for any 'polishing' that is then required by the student.

Once started, NEAs can take up a fair bit of time. It's a good idea to adjust revision plans to include a block for that subject every day, to keep on top of it.

It's a great plan to set a personal deadline a couple of weeks earlier than the real one, so that there's time to ask for feedback from their teacher (if appropriate), and for proof-reading.

There should be guidelines on the exam board website about how marks are allocated, so it's worth checking that out for each piece of NEA submitted - have they missed anything?

Essay structure

The key to a great essay is structure.

Their teachers will be able to give them a way to structure an exam question for that particular subject. It'll usually be an acronym. (For example, they might suggest they PEE on the page. That's normal, and nothing to be worried about.)

Ok, for those of you worrying anyway, PEE stands for Point, Evidence, Explain. See!

It's really easy to ramble on about something and not ever actually make a point. We've all endured our child doing a 45 minute recap of a 15 minute episode of kids' TV. Which they insist on doing, even though we watched it with them in the first place. I don't know about you, but I'm having Dora the Explorer flashbacks right now. (I believe it's an alternative form of PTSD - Post Toddler Stress Disorder....)

When they're writing an essay question, if all else fails, and using as much evidence as they can;

- Tell the examiner what they're going to tell them (introduction)

- Tell them (main bit)

- Tell them what they told them (summary/conclusion)

You can't write a great essay by accident. They take practice.

Your child needs to use past papers, homework assignments and mocks to rehearse writing great essays. They need to ask each teacher if there's a particular structure for essays in that subject, whether those are part of their NEA, or whether they're questions worth lots of marks in an exam.

They need to *learn* those structures - see the chapter on memory coming up next - and then they need to make sure they can plan and execute an essay using that structure in the amount of time they'll get in the exam.

The more chances they find to rehearse this skill in the two years leading up to their exams, the easier their exams will feel.

THE ONE THING

Get your child to check with their teachers and list out their deadlines (at least roughly - schools might not have an exact date, but they should at least know in which half term NEAs fall).

TIDYING UP YOUR BRAIN

A bit about how your memory works, and some nifty ways to memorise important things.

A man walks into the library and asks the librarian for a book on the mating habits of great white sharks[1]. The librarian pecks away at her keyboard, and says she'll have to go and fetch it. It's in the back of the library, on a very high, dusty shelf, and can only be reached by a rather wobbly ladder, so she's not impressed when he takes the book, opens it up, makes a quick note, and hands it back.

The following day, the man returns, and asks for the same book. Rolling her eyes as she walks away, the librarian retraces her steps, climbs the ladder, and returns with the book.

Again, he takes a quick look, and hands it back.

After a week of this, she's had enough. She starts leaving the book on the bottom shelf instead.

After two weeks, she's keeping the book under her desk, and is already reaching for it when he walks in.

. . .

The librarian is your brain, and the library is your memory.

That thing your teacher told you once about the battle of Hastings is a dusty old book. It's in there somewhere, but it's going to take some searching for.

However, the more you come back to that piece of information, the more important your memory realises it is, and so it reshuffles the filing system a bit to make it easily accessible.

That's why you can drive to work without thinking about which way to go.

It's why you don't have to look up the cooking instructions for your go-to meals.

It's also why you can remember your childhood phone number better than your current mobile number[2]!

When revising, the key is to get information into the long-term storage system, properly filed so you can find it again.

The key is repetition and *links*.

The more links you can make between bits of information, the better. That's why mindmaps rule.

The more you can process the information as you revise it, the more likely it is to stay off that dusty old shelf.

There are lots of great memory techniques (see Dominic O'Brien's books for example) for those that use the old 'brain like a sieve' excuse.

For lists of things:

This is a method advocated by Dominic O'Brien, in his book 'How to Pass Exams[3]'.

It is as much about imagination as it is about memory.

In summary, you take a very familiar journey - route to

school, your morning routine at home etc - and use it to memorise a list of dates/facts etc.

I'll use his example:

The royal houses of Great Britain in the order of their reigns.

1. Norman
2. Plantaganet
3. Lancaster
4. York
5. Tudor
6. Stuart
7. Hanover
8. Windsor

To link the story to the 'Royal' concept, we're setting it around Buckingham Palace.

Picture NORMAN Bates (Psycho), Greg Norman (Golf), Norman Reedus (The Walking Dead) or any other Norman who is familiar to you (Norm the robot from Phineas & Ferb is mine!) leaving the Palace through the front gates.

He has just had tea with the Queen. To remember Planta-ganet, imagine Norman stepping onto a PLANE waiting outside the gates.

The plane turns out to be a LANCASTER bomber, and as Norman takes off over London, he decides to go on a bombing raid. Instead of dropping bombs though, he's drop-ping YORKie bars. One of the giant yorkie bars crashes into the roof of a TUDOR-style house, and a Scotsman called STUART rushes out, disturbed by the commotion. He looks a bit worse for wear, and is carrying an empty bottle, telling you he's probably got a pretty bad HANgOVER.

He then is knocked over by the tide as someone WIND-SURfs past him on the street.

Crazy story, but if you add enough imagination to actually

SEE it happening, it'll stick in your head and help you remember the 8 royal houses (in order).

They can use this technique for all sorts - I helped my son to learn his Spanish verbs using this method, and have been using it myself since my dad taught it to me as a teenager!

Lists of key terms, history timelines, even formulae - it's all down to their imagination. We remember stories, so make it creative!

In the next chapter, I'll talk more about how they can use mindmaps to make links between facts and topics, and to help them remember.

THE ONE THING

Encourage your child to build up the habit of revisiting information like this:

- After 10 minutes
- After a day
- After a week
- After a month
- After three months

By that point, it should be firmly embedded!

---

1. We're not going to ask why.
2. If you're reading this 10 years after I wrote it, you need to know that when I was a kid, we had to actually memorise or write down our phone numbers. Oh, and our mums always answered the phone by repeating our number as if it was a question, because we didn't have caller id. Yes, really.
3. https://www.amazon.co.uk/How-Pass-Exams-Accelerate-Effectively/dp/1844833917/

OOOOH, A SHINY THING

The danger of distractions.

How many times have you opened up your phone to look for something, spotted a notification, and then TOTALLY forgotten what you opened your phone for in the first place?

That notification of a new email, or a text, or that your lives have refilled on Candy Crush can completely knock you off task. And, once off task, it's not so easy to get back in the zone.

When you're in the zone, concentrating, focused, it's like steaming down the motorway in your car. When you are 'distracted', it's causing your car to turn off down a slip road. The catch? There's no slip road back on. Not for a while. You're going to have to drive through a little village, stop at the traffic lights, and possibly even pull over and consult a map before you can get back on the motorway.

Studies have shown that the average time it takes to regain your concentration after a distraction is just under 25 minutes. Your brain is like a great big tanker full of knowledge, and so while it can go along pretty fast in one direction, it takes a lot of time and effort to change directions. You may *think* you can multitask, but you can't. Every time you switch tasks, your brain needs to refocus, taking valuable time. Even if you can go straight back to working after checking an email, your brain isn't working efficiently. It's not learning properly, it's not filing things properly, and it's simply slower to process.

Being 'in the zone' or 'in flow' is a powerful thing.
  Think back to the times you've got so lost in a task that hours have flown by. You may have forgotten to eat lunch, but by heck you got a lot done.

A lot of the time, distractions are a *decision*.

We *decide* to check our phone in the middle of writing that important email.
  We *decide* to leave our phone on loud so that every ping or bingle-bongle can throw us off task.
  We *decide* to try to get the big presentation written up at the office on a Friday when everyone just wants to chat.

Distractions cost us time.

One focused half-hour block of studying is worth two half-hearted *hours* of distracted studying.

If you can get the message across to your child that distractions are the enemy of their Xbox/social media time/Netflix bingeing, it will make a HUGE difference.

While I know that telling them to leave their phone in another room while they study is like telling them to chop off their own foot, they'll get so much more done, in so much less time, that it's worth the battle.

(We were so impressed with our son's levels of concentration. He could spend *hours* sat in his room revising.... Until we realised that he'd actually been lying to us and reading on his Kindle instead the whole time. Grrrr.)

Don't underestimate the siren call of social media. I joined TikTok as part of our marketing plan for the business - yes, not just for teenagers, there are lots of celebs and brands etc on there too.

I kid you not, I lost an entire day this weekend to scrolling through other people's videos and compulsively checking whether my own had got any more views or likes since I last checked 2 minutes ago.

Social Media platforms are very deliberately designed to keep you there. Scrolling. Reading. Watching.

Seriously, they have whole departments whose only job is to make their platforms *more* addictive.

. . .

If your child struggles with this, you may have to support them by setting limits or by taking their phone while they work.

NOTE: This should be done with their consent and input if at all possible. If they don't want to work, taking their phone won't make them. If they feel 'oppressed', they'll rebel. It's not worth the conflict if they're not on board.

Willpower is a funny thing.

I can decide all I like that I'm not going to snack on junk food, and as long as I'm having a good day, I can resist. It's easy.

Until something gets on my nerves, or upsets me. At that point, if there are Pringles in the house, I *will* find them.

Willpower often needs to be matched by preventative measures in order to win.

If there *aren't* any unhealthy snacks, I'm probably too lazy to go to the shops just to get some.

If my phone isn't nearby while I'm working, I'm probably too lazy to get up to check it.

If we have removed his Kindle from his room, along with anything else he could distract himself with, he's probably going to give up and revise. (True story.)

Apps like 'Moment' will tell them how many times they pick up their phone.

'Forest' starts growing a tree on their phone when they start work, and if they look at anything else on their phone while they should be studying, the tree dies. (They also plant real trees - it's a good cause.)

• • •

Their phone is likely to be their biggest source of distraction, so they need to decide how to handle that. Out of the room is best. Airplane mode is okay too. They might need you to be bad cop on this one - I refer you back to the lack of ability to make wise choices described in the introduction...

THE ONE THING

Get your child to count the number of notifications they get in the space of half an hour (ideally sometime close to when they would normally be revising. That's normally a wake-up call).

STAGE 4: DOING

MOCKS

Making the most of the opportunities they bring,
while avoiding getting too stressed out about them.

Mindset - mocks should be more helpful than stress-inducing. Here's why.

Mock exams can be incredibly helpful. They give students a chance to have a consequence-free dress rehearsal for the real things. That said, it really does depend on a student's mindset about them.

If your child is putting too much pressure on themselves over mocks, it's going to a) stress them out, b) stress *you* out and c) make them miss out on all the helpful aspects of the mocks.

The way you help them mentally 'frame' the mocks can be a game-changer.

Before any big show, there's a dress rehearsal. It is used to find all the glitches, so they can be fixed before the curtains open for real. Hat falling off during the big dance number? Hair grips. Leading actor keeps mispronouncing a word? Rewrite that line with a different word. The point is, you've got to *find the glitches* by screwing up in the dress rehearsal, or you can't fix them.

No-one expects the dress rehearsal to go perfectly. That's not what it's for.

Mocks are just a dress rehearsal.   The results don't usually make much difference, except maybe to their tier of entry (foundation / higher) in a few cases.

Here's why they're so useful:

- They can try out different revision techniques to see which work best for them.

- They can see which bits they know pretty well already, and which they need to revise.

- They can find knowledge gaps. They won't have covered everything yet, so don't panic about them!

- They can rehearse their exam technique.

- They can get used to sitting in the exam hall / being silent / writing for aaaaaaages / lining up etc. It all makes the real thing less 'new and scary'.

Warning: There is a LOT of bad advice on the internet - just search 'mock exam tips', and you'll find forums full of teenagers saying 'don't bother revising - they're just mocks'. You and I know that's bad advice, but teens tend to take whichever advice they like best...

Also, unforeseen circumstances can suddenly mean that mock grades are very important[1]. There's a balance to be found between not putting too much pressure on yourself, and still trying your hardest.

Pre-mocks - ways to prepare, things to remember.

. . .

Remember the 'cheat-sheet'. As mentioned in Stage 2, while they revise, jot down key facts / quotes / dates / formulae. Keep it as short and simple as possible - it'll have to go on an A4 sheet. They're aiming for a page of important things to remember, so they can take the page with them, and read it to themselves just before they go into that mock. It helps reduce the memorising aspect of exams. When they get in, they can even regurgitate that from memory onto the back of their answer paper or some scrap paper, so they don't have to remember it for more than about 10 minutes!

The act of condensing their revision to those few things to 'remember' is also really helpful itself - they're having to triage and choose the important vs the trivial, the bits they know vs the bits they don't, and all this is helping their brain get information filed away effectively.

Wouldn't it be great if we could read the examiner's mind?
We can't do that right now, but we can read his mind last year…

A GCSE mark scheme is like peering inside an examiner's brain. Each one shows you EXACTLY what students had to do to get the mark for each question.

Bear with me while I slip into teacher mode for a minute… (it's ok, it'll be over soon…)

You can get hold of both past papers and mark schemes online for every subject. Google '(subject) GCSE mark scheme'. (Make sure it's the right exam board.)

There are sometimes abbreviations and codes used, but there will also be a list of what they mean at the start of the mark scheme.

"If you don't show your working, you won't get the marks!"
   Every maths teacher ever

———————

Studying mark schemes will show you exactly what the examiners want you to write down to get the marks. Spending an hour or two in the few days before each exam looking at these can make a HUGE difference. It's also a great way to be clear on the structure of an exam, as well as helping with revision!

Imagine someone asked you to do your driving test again tomorrow. You've probably been driving for years, but do you remember all the little things you're supposed to do? I reckon I'd fail on minors because I've a) developed lazy habits, and b) I can't remember the 'textbook' way to do it all. I'd have to read up on 'what the examiner is looking for on your driving test', and maybe look at their marking sheet template. School exams are the same. The mark scheme shows you what things you have to include in answers to get the marks. You can find them on the exam board websites.

Google: "mark scheme (subject) (year) GCSE"

Don't just read your notes! It's one of the least effective ways to revise, but the easiest (so most tempting). They should be using their notes to create a mindmap/flashcard/synopsis/bulletpoints of key things. The more different things they try, the better. It's a great chance to try out different techniques to see what works best. They could also explain key things to you - it's a very effective way to revise!

. . .

Write, don't type. When revising, it's useful to write notes out in pen - they're going to need to be able to scribble away for at least an hour in the exam, so building up writing stamina is a good plan!

During mocks - getting every last drop of 'helpful' out of them.

Use the clock. If they have a 60 minute paper, worth 60 marks, they should be aiming for a mark a minute. If they've taken 15 minutes to answer a 5 mark question, they're going to struggle to have time to get enough marks from the rest of the paper. Seriously, cut it off, move on, and then come back at the end if they have time. They shouldn't spend ages struggling over one question.

Skip it, don't bluff it. There are going to be questions in the mock on topics they haven't covered yet. When they find one, they shouldn't try to bluff their way through, they should skip it and do the questions they *have* studied. If there's time at the end, then great, go back and have a go by all means, but don't waste time on a guess until they've completed the questions they *can* do.

Post-mocks - how to debrief a mock paper, and where to go from there.

After each exam, get them to do a debrief. (They may not thank you at the time, but they will later.)

All they need is a page with the headings:

- *topics I didn't know*
- *things I couldn't remember*
- *the hardest thing about this exam was...*
- *the easiest thing about this exam was...*

It'll help them focus their revision, and remind them when they get their results that actually they hadn't done 3 of the topics, so a grade 4 isn't actually that bad (for example). It'll also help them know which bits to add to their cheat-sheet for the real thing! They can then compare this with their paper when they get it back too.

Finally, get them to **pick a reward for when mocks are over**. However pragmatically you look at them, mocks are still a pretty intense week or two of exams and revision. It's important to have something to look forward to, whether that's a day out somewhere, or a trip to the cinema with some mates.

Mock results

As a general rule, evidenced throughout my 15 years of teaching, students will NOT be happy with their mock results.

Here's why:

- They've usually only done 66% of their GCSE study at the time they do mocks.
- They're just starting to get their heads around what GCSE exams actually *feel* like. Exam technique is a skill in itself.
- They've not usually hit their stride with revision yet. Even the keen ones often find they've been doing lots of passive revision, which hasn't quite done the job of getting information into their long-term memory.

- They haven't done many past papers yet. Schools tend to do this last, once all the 'learning' has been covered.

All these lead to mock results that are below what they expected.

Ask any teacher, and they'll tell you the most useful thing mocks do for students is scare them into starting to revise properly.

Here's how you as a parent can deal with the fallout:

Option 1: Your child has been studying hard, and is already stressed.

They have been building a strong foundation so far. If they think of it as a jigsaw puzzle, they may have put together ALL the edge pieces now. It might not look like much yet, but they're SOOOOO much closer to 'success' than the people who are still digging around for the corner pieces.

It may be that they now need to try a different approach. (There's learning and then there's revising.) Revising is about taking the information from your short-term to your long-term memory, and can mean using a different technique to the original learning.

Option 2: Your child has been avoiding revision so far.

'I told you so' won't help. It'll just make them less likely to listen to your advice. I promise.

They need to put together a revision plan, and start work. It'll involve trying out different techniques, and maybe even starting by learning to mindmap properly.. They'll have to pick what works best *for them*.

The key is to help them to see that this is *just a step along the way*.

Even if mock grades are taken into account in 6th form applications, they are always trumped by exam grades in the end.

They have time. This is a marathon, not a sprint.

If they know *why* they're working for these grades, it'll help. What difference will it make to them? *Their own reasons*, not just the ones we think are important as adults…

I've seen kids go from an F in their mocks to a C in their maths GCSE. It takes a sustained effort, but it's achieveable.

THE ONE THING

Don't put too much pressure on 'results' with mocks.
This should be about effort, and testing out their revision so far.
Mocks are a learning tool, not a judgement.

---

1. The pandemic in 2020 meant that mocks were suddenly a big part of the evidence teachers used to give a grade that year.

CRUNCH TIME

It's time. Exams are about to start, and the panic is kicking in.

Here are some key things to know.

What should they focus on?

Hopefully, they've been keeping track of which topics they've found trickiest. (The 'red' topics). Those are a great place to be revising.

As they recap the parts of the course that relate to each exam, they should keep track of which bits they're struggling to remember, and add them to a 'cheat sheet' - more on that shortly.

Double-check the exam timetable

Yes, this sounds obvious, but at this point I need to confess something.

I nearly missed my last GCSE exam.

It was English Literature, and I was convinced that it was in the afternoon. At just after 9am, the phone rang. Everyone else was out, and I was just getting up. It was school asking where the heck I was, since my exam was actually *in the morning. Now.*

PANIC!

I had to get to school for 9:30 or I'd be too late (there are rules). I ended up having to ask a friend's mum who lived down the road to drive me to school, and I was in such a tizz when I got there that they wouldn't let me start until I'd calmed down.

I didn't get to leave the exam hall with all my friends and celebrate the exams being over, since they'd long since left when I got out.

The point of my cautionary tale? Even mostly sensible people do stupid things. Don't be me.

Check the structure of the exam

Each paper needs them to do different things.

If they have a choice of questions, are they clear on which questions they *should* answer? You'd be amazed how many students try and answer questions on a book or a topic they didn't study…

It's also scarily common for students to try to answer more questions than they need to. This only applies to papers where they have to choose (usually between essay topics).

A quick check of a past paper or the specification before each exam should make it clear what they should be aiming for.

Cheat Sheet time

Now is the time for those cheat sheets we talked about earlier.

Anything they're struggling to remember, or key

facts/dates/formulae they'll need, get them all on a sheet of A4, one per exam.

While they stand outside waiting to go in, they should be studying this piece of paper intently. They'll put it away before they go into the exam hall, obviously, but as soon as they're allowed to write, they should be frantically regurgitating the whole thing onto the back of the paper or some blank paper.

That way, they should only have to remember it all for 10 minutes or so.

Sleep

Pulling an all-nighter of revision before an exam is more likely to hinder than help.

Their concentration will be better with sleep.

Their memory will be better with sleep.

Sleep is more important than last-minute revision.

Brain Food

It seems a no brainer, but eating correctly prior to an exam is vital. This is where parents really can have an impact. We do know best, despite what your teenager will say!

Put most simply, the brain needs the energy from food to work efficiently. The teenage mental focus should be on the exam, and not on the hungry noises their stomach is making. All the preparation beforehand could be undone if the brain is too fatigued to quickly recall the important information.

If there was a menu available to your teen on exam days (imagine having the time to do this!), it could look something like this…

•   •   •

Poached eggs on brown bread - eggs contain choline which boost cognitive performance.

Porridge - sweetened by honey (oats also contain choline).

Sugar-free (but don't tell them!) muesli with natural yogurt - high in fibre and helps release energy slowly to the body.

Any kind of nuts. They are all excellent brain food.

Whole grain cereals - contain fibre, vitamins, and minerals that promote slow steady release of energy to the body through a day of exams.

Fig roll biscuits - Figs contain natural sugars, and antioxidants that help protect brain cells from damage. The biscuit element contains white flour so don't let them go too crazy with them!

Wholemeal bread smeared in honey - honey is carbohydrate rich due to its fructose and glucose content, it makes a high-powered, natural energy snack.

Water, water, and more water - one of the keys to brain performance is hydration. This does come with a warning though - needing a trip to the toilet in exam time is a huge no-no. It puts the student off, takes precious time out of the exam and is distracting to those seated around you. Tactical hydration - drink when they wake up which gives them time to go to the loo prior to the start of the exam.

The importance of eating a healthy breakfast can't be overstated here. The reality of exam schedules is that in the summer, students will often have to tackle 2 and very occasionally 3 exams on the same day. Parents will need to be the ones to plan how to ensure that good brain food is eaten for lunch as well.

Basically, you're aiming for slow-release carbs, not quick-release stuff (like sugary things). No-one needs a sugar crash in the middle of an exam...

Quick Fix Stress-Busters

Laugh! When people laugh, the autonomic nervous system chills out and the heart is allowed to relax. Laughter can also boost the immune system; it has been found to increase a person's ability to fight viruses and foreign cells, and reduce the levels of three stress hormones. Whether you take 10 minutes to watch a 'try not to laugh' video on YouTube, or your fave hilarious TV moment (I can't watch Sheldon in the ballpit without cracking up every time), LAUGH!

Exercise. Just a quick stroll will do. No need for joggies or leggings even. Exercise relieves stress in several ways. First, cardiovascular workouts stimulate brain chemicals that foster growth of nerve cells. Second, exercise increases the activity of serotonin and/or norepinephrine. Third, a raised heart rate releases endorphins and a hormone known as ANP, which reduces pain, induces euphoria, and helps control the brain's response to stress and anxiety.

Reduce the distractions. Not just for general focus, but for your sanity. Constant interruptions can make us feel 'scattered'. Training yourself out of the urge to instantly respond to Snapchat / Whatsapp etc can make a HUGE difference to your day. I turned off my on screen notifications for emails and social media. It was the best decision I've made for my stress levels in a while! I still check both regularly, but it's on MY terms, not theirs.

THE ONE THING

Repeat after me... This is temporary. This is temporary. This is temporary....

STAGE 5: WINNING

TIME FOR THE HAPPY DANCE

You did it!

You all survived GCSEs intact. And you're still vaguely sane.

(If you're just reading really far ahead and your child is still at the start of Y10, then just take a minute to imagine that this is you. Breathe it all in. You'll be here soon enough.)

This is the bit where they've finished their exams, they're busy chilling in the garden with blissful amounts of nothing at all to do for weeks, and your blood pressure has dropped back to normal levels.

(However prepared you think you are, their exams are going to stress you out too. It's normal.)

. . .

There is nothing you or they can do to change their results now, so there's no point in worrying.

They need a break. Exams are full-on exhausting, and they've earned this.

You all deserve a reward. That could be a holiday, some quality family time, or whatever works for you!

When they start to get a bit bored, this *could* be a good chance to do a bit of pre-reading for their post-16 courses. It'll take some of the pressure out of Y12.

They could also just learn a new skill - I highly recommend touch-typing!

It might also be their first real chance to have a job.

Or learn to cook...

BONUS TIPS

WHAT'S NEXT?

Planning for the steps after post-16, so that they make the right choices AT post-16.
Details on the various routes available to them, and key things to know about each.

If you don't have a destination, there's no map that can help you.

While that's true, it's also true that wandering round in circles, or standing still is unlikely to help you find somewhere new and interesting.

If your child really doesn't know what they want to do, then the best thing they can do is keep as many doors open as possible.

Stick to subjects they love, sure, but make sure they

include general subjects that universities and employers value. (Like History, Philosophy, English, Economics…)

Now is a really great time to do some research on the kind of university courses they think they might be interested in, or apprenticeships that tickle their fancy, or job requirements if they think they'd like to go straight into the world of work.

If they wait until halfway through post-16 to find out that actually, the course they want to do at the university they visited requires A A B at A-level, and ignores all vocational qualifications, it could be too late.

If they find out that the apprenticeship they want to do gives priority to applicants with some kind of experience in that field, but they've already been and done their work experience in something unrelated, it'll be too late.

It's why young married couples deliberately buy houses in an area with great schools if they can. Even if they haven't had any kids yet. It's an insurance policy.

The further ahead you can plan, the better.

Here is a MONSTER section on everything you could possibly want to know about their options. Go and grab a cuppa before you start. You're going to need it.

Ahead of post-16 subject choices, there's always a lot of discussion about the varying levels of education, from 1 to 8. In a nutshell, here are the highlights.

Level 1 - GCSE level at grade 1,2, & 3.
  Level 2 - GCSE level at grades 4-9
  Level 3 - BTEC, CTEC, A level
  Level 4 - Higher National Certificates / Higher apprenticeships
  Level 5 - Foundation degrees / Higher National Diplomas
  Level 6 - University degree / Degree apprenticeship
  Level 7 - Master degree / PGCE
  Level 8 - PhD

Across the UK, roughly 31% of 18 year olds go to university. In 2018, 88% of students were offered their first choice with the remaining 12% going for their insurance offer or go through the 'clearing' system. Another fact worth considering is that students attending a 6th form are far more likely to attend university than those that chose a college based vocational option following their GCSEs[1].

If your child knows what they want to do

Brilliant - now scour the internet to find the opportunities that'll help them achieve this. If they want to go to university, start looking at course and grade requirements. These rarely change year to year, and knowing what the end game is can be very powerful in helping to motivate them.

. . .

They *need* to know what A-levels or vocation qualifications are required to get into the course they want, and what grades are needed. We've talked to SO MANY teenagers who knew exactly what they wanted to study at university, but had no clue about what it would take to get there.

If they want to explore apprenticeship opportunities, then starting to look now is a good idea. Employers will have a clear set of entry requirements and knowledge is power. Degree apprenticeships are becoming ever more popular these days due to the perceived[2] high cost of university study. Getting a job and having that employer pay for their university tuition is a genius way of staying debt free whilst earning a decent salary. These opportunities are still relatively few and far between, however.

The main reason to consider post-16 choices now is to make sure that they are doing everything they need to in order to get themselves onto the 'right' course.

What if they're not sure what they want to do?

Not a problem. 75% of graduate training schemes aren't worried about the A levels or degree that a student gets, so long as the A level results are good, and the degree isn't in Xbox Management. Companies like to take raw recruits and train them themselves.

They should choose subjects that they're interested in and achieved good grades in at GCSE.

(Only do the sciences and/or maths if they get a grade 7 or above. Grade 6's tend to end badly in those 4 subjects.)

I know I keep saying A-levels, but the same applies for all the vocational qualifications too. It's just that vocational courses are more for those who already know the sort of thing they want to do.

Degree apprenticeships - Level 6 (i.e. the same as a 'normal' degree)

Degree apprenticeships are similar to higher apprenticeships, but they provide an opportunity to gain a full Bachelor's degree or Master's degree (Level 7).

They're seen by universities as an expanding sector due to the concerns regarding the cost of going to university. (Aston University in Birmingham describe them as an integral part of their future funding.) At the time of writing, they are only available in England and Wales and it takes between 3-6 years to complete the degree aspect.

The length depends on the employer and how much time they want the employee working in the business, and how much time they want them studying for their degree. The structure of the course is always made clear in the particulars.

Benefits of degree apprenticeships

- Earn while you learn
- Usually, a job at the end of the course. It's unlikely that an employer will pay to train an employee, and then not want to retain them in their organisation once they have gained their degree.
- Enables employers to nurture and grow their own talent.
- Education is tailored to the needs of the student and the business they are working in.
- Employees are embedded in the ethos of the company from day 1.
- Suits people who learn best by integrating their

learning with the day to day hands on experience of applying what they have learned.

- If you want a degree, but not the £50k student debt, this is a good plan!

Are there any disadvantages?

- Missing out (depending on your opinion) on the social aspect of university.
- Still a limited range of vocations available through degree apprenticeships. Universities and employers are only just waking up to the huge potential of this route to a degree.
- Ties the student to their employer for a number of years while they study (this can also be seen as a huge advantage!)
- Degree apprenticeships are rigorous programmes that are not for the faint hearted. It's full time, hard work and hard study.
- There is concern over funding. At the moment there is a government sponsored pot of money to help support degree apprenticeships, but this is running out. Whether the government chooses to rectify this remains to be seen.
- Probably means leaving home once they have finished their post-16 education. (I've included this in the disadvantages list - though I'm sure some parents will disagree!)

Every apprenticeship programme is different, but there is often an up-front period of study, followed by working within the business and being expected to start adding value to that business.

If your child is sure that they don't want to study at university in the traditional sense, then this could be a perfect fit.

Open University (OU)

If going to university and having the full 'student experience' is not for your child, then the Open University is well worth considering. This will also allow them to earn while they learn. The downside to this (depending on your point of view!) is that it could guarantee that they don't move out for many, many years...

According to research, a quarter of all OU applications last year were from 18-23 year olds. This shows we are moving on from a 'traditional' approach to further education. OU courses allow you to study all the way to level 8 - a PhD!

Part time study to allow students to work is the most popular route. 18 hours of study a week offers plenty of time to be able to earn a living. Full time courses require 36 hours of study per week. The more study, the shorter the degree, obviously.

Whatever route your child wants to take after school, it is well worth starting to think about building evidence for their CV or personal statement.

No interest in a degree?

For many careers, there is absolutely no reason not to go straight into employment. At the age of 11(?!), our daughter has 'decreed it to be so' that she wants to be an interior designer and has no interest in going to university. I've no idea where she gets her strong minded, almost stubborn nature from. Honest[3].

There are plenty of apprenticeships available, or just the good old fashioned applying for a job and starting work. The pretty obvious piece of advice is to ensure their CV is as strong as it can be for a 16-18 year old. UCAS applications really need work experience on them to be considered as strong applications, and for those wanting to go straight into work, work experience placements during their post 16 education take on even greater significance. These work experiences need to be fought for. . . . they won't land on your child's lap.

Emailing and phoning local employers is an absolute must.

When it comes to convincing an employer that they should take them on for work experience, it should include the same levels of persuasion and persistence that your child uses to convince you to get them the new iPhone.

The Vocational route

1 in 4 students entering university in 2018 studied a more vocational path through A level.

You know about the the old style 'traditional' A-level subjects which have largely escaped government induced changes that included a radical (and entirely pointless in my honest opinion!) overhaul of GCSEs.

The applied A level subjects didn't survive this, so schools and colleges have instead turned to BTEC (Business and Technology Education Council) and CTEC (Cambridge Technical) courses.

The good news is that these courses count toward the all important (to the government, and nobody else!) league tables and therefore attract funding which means schools and colleges can afford to run them.

Terminal assessment is essentially what happens on the traditional A level subjects. You work hard for 2 years and (sweeping generalisation coming . . . .) 2 exams of two and a half hours decide your entire grade.

This method of assessment is clearly not going to be helpful to students who struggle with this 'remember everything in one go' approach.

The BTEC/CTEC (better known as vocational courses) are typically structured like this:

Unit 1 of 90 hours of teaching - exam at the end

Unit 2 of 90 hours teaching - exam at the end

Unit 3 of 60 hours teaching - coursework or exam (the teacher gets to choose)

Unit 4 of 60 hours teaching - coursework assessed by the class teacher

Unit 5 of 60 hours teaching - coursework assessed by the class teacher

. . .

Of the 360 hours (the usual requirement of a post 16 course) half is exams and half is coursework. Typically the 2 years may look like this:

Year 12 - take one exam in May of year 12, complete 2 courseworks over the year.

Year 13 - take the other exam in Jan of Yr 13 and complete the final coursework. With only 2 units to complete, it leaves room to study for exam retakes in the summer of year 13.

All exams can be taken twice, and the best score counts[4].

Near pass is a winner for those who struggle with exams

Students with learning difficulties are quite often brilliant at coursework and can achieve excellent grades on half of the course. Particularly with the CTEC courses, the examined parts are now graded at Distinction, Merit, Pass, and Near Pass.

The near pass was introduced because it quickly became obvious that students with learning difficulties who struggle with exams were failing the course despite having really good coursework marks.

In the 5 unit example above, if the student gets a near pass in the 2 exams and distinctions in the 3 coursework units, then an overall Merit is awarded - the equivalent of a 'C' at A level.

In short - students who take the vocational route can get good grades if they put the hard work in. If they then choose to go onto further study at university, then these vocational qualifications are welcomed with open arms.

Imelda (name changed, obviously) studied a mix of CTEC and BTEC in ICT, Business Studies, and Science. She was predicted merits across the board despite being poor at exams due to a range of learning difficulties. She applied to 5 universities (see list below) to study a business management degree and received 5 unconditional offers. She achieved Distinction, Merit, Merit for her 3 subjects.

Nottingham Trent

Leeds Metropolitan

De Montfort in Leicester

Northampton

Lincoln

To give a clearer picture, her personal statement and reference were epic, which always helps.

THE ONE THING

Get your child to take some time to do the research on this.
Do they fancy a vocational route? An apprenticeship?
If they're looking at a university course, what are the grade requirements?

----

1. (source: ucas.com)
2. university study is free if you never earn over £27,000 per year.
3. I'm lying. It's from me. But you guessed that.
4. There are huge variations, of course, but this gives you a good idea.

SOCIAL MEDIA

A word of warning about something that could destroy their chances of getting their dream job

Schools should have been delivering online safety education since early in primary school. It's the sort of topic that students in years 10-13 are bored of.

Been there, heard it, it's fine, I'll behave myself.

Or so they say. . .

Sadly, the data shows that as students approach the end of their formal schooling, more and more are putting themselves on a collision course with their future employers. This doesn't only affect the world of work, but also further education. If they make mistakes (see list further down) then it could have repercussions from their university or apprenticeship sponsors.

One of the first recorded cases of an employee getting into hot water (he got fired!) was in 2005. Someone who worked for high street bookseller Waterstones posted on his blog about his employer 'Bastardstones' and an evil boss he worked for. It was a short journey to the job centre once the blog was found by the company.

From that case onwards, companies have moved to have comprehensive social media policies in place that teenagers need to know about.

It's not just their online behaviour once employed, it's their online behaviour **now**, and in the **past**.

Your child should be aware of the phrase social media foot-print, and now is the time to double check there's nothing that's going to result in that dreaded disciplinary letter from the HR department.

In fact, it could be worse, because social media misuse could result in a company not offering a position in the first place.

There's a lot of research available about how employers use social media to vet their prospective and current employees.

. . .

70% of employers use social media to 'research' candidates, with a further 7% planning to start using this tactic.

43% of companies use social media to check on current employees.

Top reasons for employers taking action over social media posts from the past or present:

Posting about alcohol or drug misuse

Posting discriminatory comments about race, sexuality, gender, religion

Posting about criminal behaviour

Bad mouthing friends

Poor communication skills

Bad mouthing previous employees/employers

Unprofessional social media account name

Sharing confidential information about a previous employer

Lying about an absence from work

Inappropriate photographs or videos

Top reasons why employers might like a candidate's social media profile.

Posts show that candidate is creative

Demonstrates a wide range of interests

Post interesting content

Demonstrate good communication skills

Other people post nice things about the candidate.

It's worth pointing out that as many as 47% of employers will only consider an application where they can find evidence of a candidate online. So hiding from social media, or having heavily disguised account names might come back to bite them too.

THE ONE THING

To many teenagers, this might be 'whatevs' and they will shrug and assure you that you have nothing to worry about. It's worth asking them to go through and check all their posts would be allowed to be showed to their gran (or other super scary sensible adult). I always use my mother in law as my measure. If I know I'll get in trouble with her, I don't post it - simple!

BRAIN FOOD

It's pretty clear that a hearty meal on the morning of the first exam isn't going to turn anyone into Einstein, but a sustained effort to eat the right food in the build up to the exams is going to make a positive difference. The build up to mocks is the best time to start this. Remember, your child need never know why you're doing this!

Foods to target

Broccoli - rich in vitamin K which is known to enhance cognitive function.

Nuts - particularly walnuts. These contain mood enhancing serotonin - could be pretty important by the end of each exam!

Sage - contains chemicals linked to improved memory and concentration.

Pumpkin seeds - rich in zinc which is vital for the thinking function of your brain.

Blackcurrants - rich in vitamin C, which increases mental agility.

Blueberries - help boost short term memory. This is really

helpful with any last minute cramming that may have happened.

Tomatoes - contain lycopene which is great for your brain

Oily fish - contain 'essential fatty acids' for healthy brain function. Salmon and mackerel are best.

Extra virgin olive oil - contains monounsaturated fat that is linked to better memory and cognitive function.

Avocados - contain monounsaturated fat, but also contain chemicals that help your brain stay motivated and focused. Avocado also helps improve blood flow to the brain.

Turmeric - long story short, it stimulates the production of new brain cells, and helps repair damaged ones.

Wholemeal crackers with houmous dip - Houmous is a great source of plant based protein, fibre and energy. It also contains olive oil and sesame seeds. It's practically a superfood.

Chewing gum - some schools ban this, but there is research that shows this boosts accuracy and assists with concentration. Mint flavour when inhaled acts as a type of smelling salt for the brain. Maybe just when revising or prior to exams, rather than run the risk of loud chewing in an exam though...

Peppermint sweets - this helps with memory and concentration. Be warned though, too many will adversely impact on the stable supply of energy mentioned earlier. Strike the right balance. Oh, and some of them can have a laxative effect if you eat too many...

Rosemary Essential oil - this is for the super keen parent! Sniffing (not eating!) rosemary essential oil can improve cognitive speed, accuracy, and mood while reducing feelings of anxiety. All winners in an exam.

Foods to avoid

- Anything made from white flour. Cakes, biscuits, anything white pasta based. The fact is the body requires additional energy to digest these and this energy will detract from the energy available for the brain to answer difficult questions. It's all about marginal gains, and this is probably the only area where we as parents can help on exam day - apart from the emotional support of course.
- Anything high in refined sugar - sweets, chocolate etc. Sugar highs and lows are not what the brain needs to work well in an exam. A stabilized energy supply is best.
- Turkey sandwiches - random, but true. Turkey meat contains chemicals that make you sleepy . . . which explains the last 40 (ish) years of Christmas afternoon naps for me!
- Sugary drinks. Energy drinks are terrible for the sugar high/low issues. Don't be fooled by any added vitamins claimed on the packaging. They are bad for your body. Full stop!
- Sugary coffee or tea. Caffeine is okay, but the sugar is not.
- Don't avoid caffeine, but DO AVOID caffeine withdrawal. If they have a cup of tea or coffee in the morning, then stick with this routine.
- Alcohol - this shouldn't need to be on the list of what a 16 year old should avoid consuming, but just in case! Alcohol impairs neurotransmission - it slows you down. We know this as adults, but students need to understand this too. This is more of an issue for A-level age students, but it's worth mentioning!

Best Snacks
Protein bars
Granola bars
Packets of nuts or dried fruit
Dark chocolate - but in small quantities

Other advice

Not many teenagers eat a healthy diet. No matter how hard we all try as parents, there is a lot of time where they're on their own, near a shop - probably eating rubbish.

A course of multivitamins starting a month prior to the exams will boost brain function and increase the body's ability to deal with stress.

It's tough to get enough water without making a conscious effort. There are plenty of water bottles designed to give you a nudge in the right direction, but really anything will do. Keep an eye on what they're drinking over the next few days. Is it water/squash/coffee or tea (in moderation), or are they going for the energy drinks and fizz option? Do they even take a drink with them, or is it just whatever they buy at lunch?

Is there anything you or they could do to help them set a good water-drinking habit now?

THANK YOU

If you've found this book helpful, will you write me a review on Amazon please?

Reviews mean a lot to authors - I can guarantee you there *will* be a happy dance here EVERY time!

You can do that on Amazon: Leave a review

If you're at the end of the book, but the start of your journey, remember - you don't have to do this on your own.

While there's a ton of useful stuff here in the book, if you feel like it would help to have someone to (metaphorically) hold your hand all the way through this, that's what our membership is for. We break all this down into weekly chunks, so it's super-simple, and doesn't require a lot of time. It's also a great way to open up the lines of communication between you and your child. (They are preprogrammed not to listen to their parents, but with the membership, the advice is coming from *us*, not you!)

I'd love to hear your stories/challenges/wins too!

Drop me a message on our Facebook page or at emily@parentguidetogcse.com